Diary of a Rescued Cat

Diary of a Rescued Cat

From being thrown in a
dumpster to the luckiest
cat in the world!

Lola and Dawn White

The Silloway Press
Beaverton, OR

Lola: Diary of a Rescued Cat
From being thrown in a dumpster to the luckiest cat in the world!

Copyright 2015 by Dawn White
All rights reserved.

Cover design by Mudpuddle Creations. http://MudpuddleCreations.com

Printed in the United States of America.
ISBN: 978-0-9831552-5-6
Library of Congress Control Number: 2014944377

10% of the proceeds from sales of this book will go to support animal rescue groups and shelters.

Contact the publisher at:
The Silloway Press: phone 301-335-9368; email: Lola@SillowayPress.com
http://SillowayPress.com

Dawn's Dedication

This book is dedicated to the memory of my grandmother, Ruth Davenport, who always told me she believed I would some day write a book.

Lola's Dedication

This book is dedicated to all the rescued animals and their humans who saved them, gave them good homes, lots of love, and a second chance at life. But most of all it is dedicated to Leslie Kaufman. Leslie saw me in the shelter and so bravely saved me—not knowing what to do with a sick cat like me, and with no place to take me but to her vet. Without her, I would not be here to tell my story. Thank you, from the bottom of my heart.

Dawn's Acknowledgments

I couldn't have done this without the support and encouragement of many people. I would like to express my deepest appreciation and gratitude to the following:

To those who read early versions (each a little different), your feedback was so helpful and pushed me to continue.

To Colleen Fishter, who encouraged me from day one to finish this book, and who read and edited (and honestly critiqued) several first drafts; and to Sean Coleman for his technical support, for making Lola's official logo, and designing our website. (Sean can be contacted via his website, www.seancoleman.com.) I promise that Lola and Lexy will do their best to carry on CQ's Caturday Night Meow legacy and make him proud.

To Peg Silloway (a fellow cat lover) and everyone at The Silloway Press, my gratitude for their guidance and patience throughout this project with a novice like me and for helping to make it happen. Thank you for taking on my project.

To all of the contributors who chose to share their personal and heartfelt stories with me, I extend my deepest appreciation. I am honored you allowed your pets to be a part of this book.

I value all of Lola's and Lexy's followers on Facebook who have supported us for the past three-and-a-half years and for giving me a reason to continue to share their photos and antics with you.

I would like to recognize the "pet community" on Facebook. I think we're pretty amazing.

To Leslie Kaufman: thank you, thank you, thank you for allowing me to adopt Lola, and for your continued friendship.

And most of all, I'd like to thank Lola and Lexy for choosing me to be their person. You fill my life with more joy than I can express.

Many thanks to you, the reader, for choosing to pick up this book and read it. I hope you continue to follow Lola's and Lexy's lives on:

Facebook (https://www.facebook.com/LolaTheRescuedCat),
Twitter (https://twitter.com/Lola_RescuedCat),
Pinterest (http://www.pinterest.com/lolarescuedcat/),
Instagram (Lola _Rescued_Cat),
and on our website: www.LolaTheRescuedCat.com.

Lola's Acknowledgments

I would like to thank all of my Facebook friends who have supported our page and encouraged me to write my life story. I have to thank Dr. Plotnick and everyone at Manhattan Cat Specialists for being so nice to me and for taking such great care of me. Thank you, Janice Rossel, for caring enough about me to take my photo while I was in the shelter, and for taking me out of my cage and showing me a moment of kindness (which you do for so many other animals in the shelter as well). I also want to thank all of the volunteers and staff at shelters everywhere whose hearts are big enough to show unwanted animals kindness and love. And of course I have to thank Aunt Leslie. And Lexy, too.

Dawn's Note

I come from a family of cat lovers, and I can remember having a cat in the house most of my life. We had Friskie, Tabitha, Morris, Samantha, and the love of my life, Marvin. Marvin was a black and white with a smudge on his nose that came to us when I was 19 and he was eight weeks old. Marvin was my sidekick, my baby, my friend; he was a constant in my life, which was full of changes. When I was 31, due to life circumstances, I had to move and was not able to take Marvin with me. Needless to say, I was devastated and not having him with me left a hole in my heart and my life that I thought would never be filled.

For the next 16 years I always lived in places that did not allow pets, so I never had to think about having one. Then one day in April 2010, I was in a pet store with my family buying supplies for my niece's new puppy and I spotted the adoption table. I saw a beautiful black-and-white cat named Lexy who reminded me of my Marvin, and it was pretty much love at first sight. I was told she had been there for nearly a year because people thought she was too old (at nearly two) or wanted more exotic looking cats. One week later, I went back to pick her up to bring her to her forever home. It was the best decision I ever made.

After eight months, I decided Lexy needed a companion (and who can have just one cat, anyway?) and began looking for another rescue. I was on Facebook one night looking for someone who could help me trap a stray that had been living behind my building when I came across the page for a cat-sitting business in my town. Since I needed a sitter, I decided to look over the page and came across Lola's picture. "Who could be so heartless as to throw an animal in a dumpster?" I wondered. She looked pathetic, sick, and neglected, but there was something in Lola's eyes that drew me to her immediately. A few days later, I stopped by the vet where she was being medically cared for just to show support. Well, one cannot possibly be immune to Lola's charms, and 5 minutes later I had adopted this 3.4 pound skinny cat with a face full of mucus who was so sick and weak she couldn't even meow. That was the second best decision I ever made.

Lola's transition from the ill, weak, fearful animal she was into the beautiful, friendly, curious feline she is today has amazed me, and it is an honor to have been a part of her journey. From the moment I brought her home, I doted over her, nursing her back to health, day and night. For several months she was the focal point of my life (but don't worry, Lexy was never ignored in any way!), and we developed a strong bond. She also developed an equally strong bond with my boyfriend, who was as devoted to her recovery as I was. Little by little she started to trust me, life, and the world more and more. She stopped running and hiding when I would come through the front door and started to await my arrival in the entrance way. Little noises that would send her under the bed or the radiator for indefinite periods of time began to be ignored as if they didn't even occur. I was able to move her feeding station from the security of the bathroom to the living room, and now she will eat in the open. (She still does not like to eat in the kitchen because of the noises of pots and pans and cooking, but she will have part of her breakfast in the kitchen window while watching the birds and the trees.) She even greets strangers, welcoming them into our home. She has definitely come a long way.

I think what amazes me most about Lola is the genuine love she shows for people. From the very moment she was rescued, she never stopped giving an abundance of love to others and couldn't receive enough of it. Whatever she went through, no matter how sick she was, she never stopped loving. That has been an inspiration to me, and at times I need to stop and remind myself of the lesson she has taught me—that no matter how bad things get, love can make them better.

I've tried my best to portray Lola as the sweet cat she is and to describe the love she demonstrates, but in reality there are no words to illustrate this. There are times when she relentlessly insists upon snuggling, hugging, and kissing, and no matter what I do, I cannot manage to stop her from licking me or manage to put her down. She is persistent and unrelenting in her quest to show her love, gratitude and appreciation for her life and her family.

Adopting two rescue cats has changed my life in many ways. They have brought so many wonderful, loving people into my life that I am so blessed to call my good friends—friends I never would have met otherwise. Because of them I am part of a wonderful pet community on Facebook that consists of so many kind, caring, generous, good-hearted people. The love and support that is found there is amazing. Becoming involved in animal rescue issues has brought to my attention the mistreatment so many animals endure, which has led me to become a vegetarian and to focus on buying cruelty-free products as much as I can.

And then there's the unconditional love that Lola and Lexy show me every day in every way. They make my house a home. I get angry when I think of someone dumping these two beautiful creatures, but then I remember that they are safe, happy, and healthy now in their forever home with me. I can't imagine my life without them.

A note about Lola's early days: I've pieced together her pre-adoption life from posts people made about her on Facebook, bits of information people told me, and documents from the shelter. I'm lucky to have this information, because I do feel her story helps to shed some light on what happens to neglected or abused animals. On our Facebook page (Lola the Rescued Cat), we have held auctions and fundraisers to help others who need assistance with rescue or veterinary care. Because of this, 10 percent of the proceeds from the sale of this book will be donated to animal rescue groups and shelters.

This book starts with Lola's story, moves on to Lexy's story, and concludes with heartfelt stories about other rescued pets. When I was sure I wanted to include this information, I posted a request on our Facebook page and received all of the sincere submissions you will read in that section.

I urge people not to buy pets and to please rescue and adopt. What you get in return is priceless. I hope Lola's story inspires you to do so.

Lola's Note

Hi, I'm Lola, and I'm a very lucky cat. My life definitely took a turn for the worse when I was thrown away in a garbage dumpster in East Harlem when I was only six months old. But I'm not garbage. I'm important and I matter, and I have a voice that needs to be heard. After someone took me out of the dumpster, I ended up in the shelter where I got very sick. But I was lucky because I found a fairy godmother who saved me and made sure I got a wonderful life. But not all animals in the shelter have a fairy godmother. I'm just lucky.

I'm here to shed light on what happens to some cats when they are abandoned or end up in a kill shelter, and also to let people know the happiness a rescued pet can bring into your life. I want to encourage people to adopt a pet from a shelter or a rescue and to treat all animals with respect and love. Rescued pets are the best breed! Don't buy a pet, adopt one!

This is my story....

Sections

Diamond
Larry
Smoky
Sadie Mae McFlufferson
Althea
Tova
Maddie Belle

Abandoned

East Harlem, New York City
Behind a housing project

Hey! Where are you taking me? Where are we going? It's cold outside! I don't like it out here! Take me back inside! Please? Oh no, what are you doing? That thing looks scary! No, don't open it, it's scary! Don't put me in there! Please, I promise I'll be good, I promise! I'm sorry for whatever I did; I didn't mean to make you angry. Please take me back inside? Oh no! (Slam). Oh no, it's dark in here, and it's smelly, and I'm really, really scared. Meoww!! Can anyone hear me? Meooowww!! Oh please, someone take me out, I don't like it in here. I hear someone...hello? Meow? Meoowww? Oh thank you, thank you for opening that lid.

"What's in there?"

"It's a cat."

"A cat? Who would put a cat in a dumpster? Take it out."

Yes, please take me out! I'm very friendly, you'll see. I'll even purr for you.

"What should we do with it?"

Take me home! I'll be a good kitty.

"We can take it to the pet store. They have cats for adoption there."

Meow. Where are we going? I'm so scared.

"We just found this cat in a dumpster. Can you take it?"

"Leave her here; we'll take care of her."

"You're such a cute cat, what were you doing in a dumpster?"

Lady, trust me, you don't wanna know.

"Well, you'll have to go to the shelter and get a work up before we can put you up for adoption."

Shelter? What does that mean? I thought I would stay here with her and now... what does it mean?! What did I do to deserve this?

December 16, 2010

Today was the worst day of my life. I was thrown away, just like that, in a smelly dumpster behind the building. That's just mean, especially since I'm only six months old. I'm still a baby! Sigh....

Well, here I am in the shelter, where they gave me an animal ID number and named me Lola. My name isn't Lola, but they don't understand what I'm meowing when I'm trying to tell them my real name. The lady who named me is nice to me, so I'll let her call me Lola. I'm warm and I have a bowl of food, but I don't like this cage. I don't like this place. I want my home.

Boy, they poked me and felt me all over the place (even in my private parts!) and looked at my teeth and took blood. I heard someone say I have to be "fixed." Fixed? I'm not broken! What are they talking about? I'm so confused.

December 20, 2010

Today someone came and took me out of my cage and put me in a little box. When I popped my head out, I was in a doctor's office and I had a feeling something not good was going to happen. First they stuck me with needles to give me vaccines, put a microchip in my neck, and then my belly got shaved. How embarrassing! And the doctor wrote down that I'm a year old. Hello! I'm six months old, thank you very much. Then they stuck a needle in my paw and I got very sleepy and took a nap. When I woke up I had stitches in my belly, so I guess they fixed whatever was broken. I don't like this place and I want to go home.

December 24, 2010

I heard the humans say today is Christmas Eve. I don't think Santa is going to come to this place. I think all of us kitties here are forgotten. I'm so confused. I can't figure out what I did to deserve this. I was always such a good kitty and I'm so lovable. Why didn't they like me? Achoo! Uh oh, I think I'm catching a cold.

December 26, 2010

Achoo! Achoo! Oh boy, this cold is getting worse. They started giving me medicine today to make me better. I heard someone say I couldn't go to "adoptions" until I'm better. I have to work real hard at that so I can find a home and get out of this place.

December 30, 2010

My cold is worse. I haven't been eating much because I can't smell my food and I'm so cold! I wish I could have a blanket. Achoo! Oh darn, every time I sneeze I get mucus all over my face. Sigh.... Should I just give up?

January 3, 2011

I think I've lost some weight. I still don't eat much and I'm just too sick to care. Today I realized that sometimes cats are taken out of their cages and never come back. I meowed at the cat next to me and asked him where they go, and he told me sometimes cats go to their new forever homes, but most are on "Death Row" and are put to sleep. Put to sleep? What does that mean? I'm so confused.

There's a sweet woman here who takes me out of my cage and sings to me while she pets me on her lap. She's so nice to me. Maybe I should ask her if she wants to be my forever mom.

January 4, 2011

Today a nice lady named Janice came in and she had a camera with her. The cat next to me told me she takes pictures of some of us to try to help find us homes. I tried to meow so loud so she would notice me, but only a squeak came out. But guess what? She saw me anyway! And she took this picture of me:

I know I don't look my best, but maybe, just maybe, someone will like me. Janice

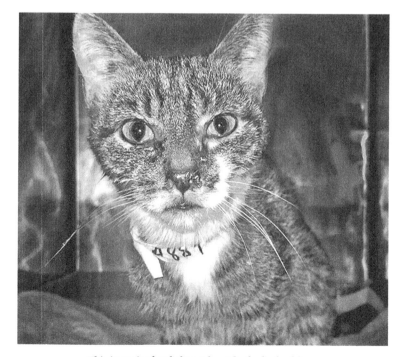

This is me in the shelter when I had a bad cold.

3

even took me out of my cage and let me sit on her lap. And guess what? She even wrote about me on Facebook. This is what she said:

> *"When meeting Lola in the Sick Ward, I knew I had to get this sweet, sweet thing out of the shelter ASAP! I believe it's a matter of life and death for her. Opening her kennel door, I removed her frail little body and put her in my lap where she so very happily remained, all the while looking up at me so pathetically with her caked nose and squinty eyes. I imagined she was pleading with me to take her from this place or maybe thanking me for showing her some kindness. It didn't take much imagination to see that. So, that's my mission folks, to try and introduce Lola to you; for you to hear something of her story and maybe, just maybe help set her free. Judging from her abandonment, it's easy to see how maligned this sweet baby has been. She may never have known what love or kindness is, like so many others here but still, she knows how to take it and to give it."*

How special is that?

Someone else wrote about me on Facebook, too. They said I was abandoned in a housing project dumpster and I don't look like garbage! They said I was one year old (I'm not one year old, why do humans keep saying that?), friendly, and available. My behavior was rated "mild." They also said I was supposed to be featured in an upcoming adoption event but got sick with an upper respiratory infection (they called it a "URI") and so I couldn't be included.

I'm keeping my paws crossed that someone will love me and take me home.

January 5, 2011

A lady came in today and was looking at me in my cage while she was asking the worker questions about me. I'm not on Death Row, but the worker told her not to wait too long. Oh no, that doesn't sound good at all. I look really bad today. My eyes are crusted over and my face and whiskers are covered with mucus and food. I look like a hot mess. Sigh…. How could this lady ever think I'm cute enough to take home? Paws crossed so I can escape Death Row.

Rescued

January 6, 2011

Today was an exciting day! A worker came to my cage to take me out and put me in a box. I got real scared because I thought I was going to be put to sleep. I couldn't see out of the box so I didn't know what was going on. I heard a lot of humans talking, and the next thing I knew I was in a car. Imagine that! A car! A little while later I finally got to come out of the box and I couldn't believe it—I was in a different doctor's office. "Oh boy, here we go again" I thought. I looked up—and there was the lady that was asking about me yesterday! But she was crying, and that made me nervous.

Everybody was fussing over me and saying things like "poor baby" and "what a shame." The doctor came in to look at me and had a list of stuff he had found wrong: I only weigh 3.2 pounds, I have a bad URI and a broken canine tooth, and I'm dehydrated and hypothermic. And my nose is really sore and it started to bleed when they cleaned it. The vet tech force-fed me with a syringe. I didn't like that very much, but she said I have to eat to get strong. Everyone here is so kind to me, and it smells a whole lot better than it did at the shelter. I have a whole room to myself, too. So now I'm going to turn in for the night and cuddle up to my snuggly warm heating pad and not have to worry about "Death Row." That lady who took me from the shelter is my fairy godmother.

January 8, 2011

Wow! I'm a popular cat! Not only does everyone here at the hospital fuss over me like I'm a newborn kitten, but I also get visitors! The lady who saved me from the shelter (I found out her name is Leslie and she owns On All Fours Cat Sitting) visits me every day, and she brings a friend named Samantha with her, too. I feel so special. I also found out that the name of this hospital is Manhattan Cat Specialists and my doctor is Dr. Plotnick. Leslie said I'm in the best hands here with them. This lady named Tamar came to visit me, too. She has a popular blog and a Facebook page named I Have Cat, and she came to see little old me! I felt very special because she came to spend time with me on her birthday. That was so thoughtful of her! There's only one problem; Leslie can't take me home to live with her because she has two cats already and her male cat doesn't get along with other cats. He's an "alpha." Darn. I thought I had a home. But Leslie is trying to find me a new family and posted this on Facebook today: "Anyone interested in adopting Lola?" She even offered to go to my new home and give me my medicine twice a day to help out. She said she'd do anything. I hope someone wants me because I don't want to go back to that shelter.

Adopted

January 9, 2011

A lady named Dawn came to visit me today. I was very excited and I tried to look stunning, but this was the best I could do:

I laid on the charm though! I gave her snuggles and the silent meow (well, I don't have any other meow besides the silent meow; I hope my voice comes back some day) and was just the sweetest little thing. She commented on how skinny I am (which made her very sad) and said

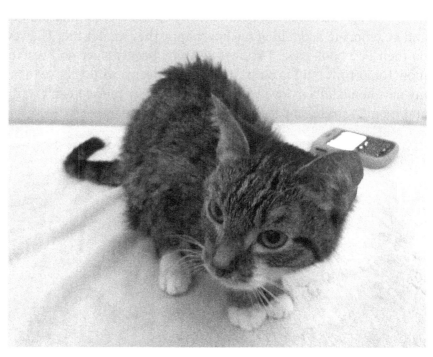

This is me the first day Mommy met me. She thought I was beautiful.

how much she loves my long elegant tail. She didn't even mind when I rubbed my snotty nose on her. Guess what she said next? She said "I had to meet you to see if I thought you would get along with my Lexy. I would love to give you a home if they will let me." She wants to be my new mom! I'm so happy I'm going to have a home and a family. Leslie has to check her references first, but I just know everything will work out. She fell in love with me already!

January 11, 2011

Guess what? Aunt Leslie (I call her Aunt Leslie now) said Dawn checked out and can be my mom! This is so awesome and I'm so excited. There's other news, too: I have a Facebook page. It turns out so many people were following my story and wanted my updates that my new mom had to start a page. I'm going to be famous, but most importantly, I'm going have a forever home with a family, complete with a sister. I hope she likes me.

January 15, 2011

I'm going home tomorrow! Everyone here at Manhattan Cats is fussing over me and hugging me and telling me how happy they are for me. They even posted about me on their Facebook page. I know I need my beauty sleep so I can look good for my new mom tomorrow, but I'm so excited I won't sleep a wink. I have to make sure everyone in my new home falls in love with me so I can stay there. I can't wait to have a comfy bed and room to stretch my legs. And a family to love me.

The Sick Room

January 16, 2011

This was the most exciting day ever! Aunt Samantha came to say goodbye to me and wish me luck in my new home. A little while later Mommy came to pick me up. She came with her boyfriend, Will, and he's a nice guy. (And if he came with her, that means he likes cats!) When Mommy was standing at the reception desk, she heard a cat meowing and meowing. She looked around, but there were no other cats there. "Is that Lola?" she asked and was so surprised to find out I could meow again! And you won't believe this... a lady named Julie was there, and when she heard my name, she said "Is that Lola the Rescued Cat?" She knew who I was! Mommy let me stick my head out of the carrier so she could meet me, but I tried to make a run for it, so back in I went. Julie is one of my Facebook friends. I can't believe I have friends and people who care about me.

When we got to my new home, I smelled a cat but I didn't have a chance to see it because Will rushed me off to the bathroom. I'm still sick, so I have to be separated for a while. I heard Mommy say, "They'll have to be introduced slowly".

So far I like Mommy. She gives me hugs and lets me give her face rubs. She even made me a little blankie so I'm not cold. Isn't that super? And she doesn't get upset that I have diarrhea. She just picks up the rugs and puts towels down on the floor for me.

Wow, I can't believe I have my own bed, and I can walk around and not have to live in a cage anymore. I lived in a cage for 31 days and it wasn't fun. Tonight when I sleep in my bed I'm going to pray that all the cats on Death Row be saved just like I was.

January 17, 2011

Day two in my new home. I'm a little weak today and tired, so I just lay in my bed for a while. Mommy says she will get me well if it's the last thing she does. She loves me, and that makes me feel so good! Sigh...it's great being rescued.

My second day in my forever home.

January 19, 2011

Big news! Last night I jumped **FROM THE FLOOR** onto Mommy's lap! That is something, considering I could hardly get into my bed when I first came. I never saw Mommy so surprised. (OK, I know I haven't known her that long, but still.) She's hoping today will bring a new miracle for me as well. Oh, and I ate A LOT last night!

Meeting My New Sister

January 20, 2011

Lexy scares me. At night she sounds like a mountain lion, stalking me on the other side of the bathroom door! She growls and hisses, and growls some more. I think she may want to eat me. I can't believe all that comes out of this sweet little face.

January 22, 2011

Today I saw Lexy face to face for the first time. Earlier today, Mommy and Will let us see each other through a crack in the bathroom door. Lexy hissed once, but I

My new sister, Lexy.

hissed a few times and growled and swatted at her. A little while later they put Lexy in the bathroom and let me walk around the living room and kitchen. It's a pretty cool place with lots of places to hide. But all of a sudden other people in the building made a lot of noise in the hallway, so I ran and hid under the radiator, and Mommy got me out.

I haven't seen the outside world in so long!

I even looked out the window for a minute. I haven't seen the outside world in such a long time! There were no birds flying around, though, so I jumped down. I even played with Lexy's catnip mouse! After exploring a little while longer, it was back to the bathroom (which I call the Executive Suite now).

Mommy and Will decided a while later to bring me out again, first in the carrier and then, since everything seemed cool, they let me out. Lexy was watching me and didn't like it very much when I sat next to Mommy. Well, she's my Mommy, too! I didn't quite know what to do with myself, so I walked around a little. When I got too close to Lexy's space, she growled so I went back to the Executive Suite. I think I'll see Lexy again tomorrow. I'll update on the latest gossip then.

What is that thing sitting next to my mother?

January 23, 2011

Well, today was interesting. I'll break it down into four steps:

1. Again, Will and Mommy let Lexy and me change places. I stayed out in the living room for a while and it was fun until a noise scared me and I ran under the couch. Will went in to check on Lexy at one point and she was lying in my bed. Imagine that! But after an hour, I had to go back to my suite.

2. A while later I was brought out in the carrier and Lexy eyed me up and down. I hissed and growled at her so Mommy brought me back to my suite. She figures at this point it's better not to bring me out in the carrier because I feel trapped, so she brought me back out free as a bird. There was some hissing and a little growling, and every time one of us made a sudden movement the other hissed, but guess what? We were able to stay in the same room for 30 minutes! A couple of times I got myself in a corner and Mommy got me out because she doesn't want anyone to get cornered. I mostly stayed on the couch though. After 30 minutes, back I went.

3. Mommy opened the door to my suite and out I ran! She said I'm a sneaky little devil! I ran up onto the couch and started snuggles with Will and Mommy.

Lexy looked at me as if to say "This thing again?" but we were kinda nice to each other. I heard a LOUD noise in the hallway and ran back to my suite and into the tub to hide! (It really stinks going through a scary experience. It's terrible to have your whole world turned upside down and have to start all over. And it makes me really, really scared—of almost everything!).

4. Let's just say that the third time wasn't a charm. Mommy brought me back out for one more try and there was more hissing this time around. Mommy said it was much ado about nothing. I think I stayed out for about 20 minutes. I mostly stayed on the couch.

Snuggle time with Will.

13

So that was day two of introductions. When Mommy came into the Executive Suite to check on me, I was meowing and scratching at the door to get out. Mommy said she was done for the day so I couldn't go back out. Mommy will be home late tomorrow, so Will is coming over to cat sit. I hope Lexy is nicer and doesn't look like she wants to eat me. Mommy said she never had a problem introducing cats before, but Lexy and I are different. We're both shelter cats who went through traumatic experiences, and that makes a difference.

January 24, 2011

I think today went pretty well. When Will came to check on us, he let me out for about 15 minutes but he couldn't watch us and fix his dinner at the same time, so I couldn't stay out very long. But when Mommy came home I came out again. Still some hissing going on and Lexy and I swatted at each other once, but this time I got to stay out for an hour and a half! When Mommy went into the bathroom, I ran out again! She said she can't believe how quick I am. I only stayed out a few minutes because I was trying to bother Lexy when she was using the litter box, and Mommy said that probably wasn't a good idea.

I usually spend most of my time sitting on the couch just watching Lexy, but I walked around a lot today to check things out. When Lexy gets too close to me, I hiss and maybe growl—she's so much bigger than me! Mommy thinks it's funny that anywhere Lexy goes she looks so small next to other cats, but next to me she looks like a Mountain Lion! Sometimes Lexy just ignores me, as long as I'm not in her personal space. I think we're making progress!

When Mommy came in to feed me, I was meowing and scratching at the door to get out. I even gave her the silent meow with the sad eyes, but she didn't give in. She said when we can play nice I can stay out forever, but for now I'm stuck in here. I'm really getting tired of being in here and I want to run around my new house. (Mommy thinks I'm going to be a naughty cat. I'll keep her—and my Facebook friends—guessing for now.)

Learning to Get Along

January 25, 2011

My big sister is hard to win over. Mommy came home early from work to spend time with us (and to do her laundry). She gave us both a talking to and said it's time to stop the nonsense and get along. When I came out into the "real world," Lexy and I actually went 10 minutes before we started any hissing—just a little here and there, nothing too major, but Mommy still had to keep an eye on us. She just knew Lexy was

Face to face with Lexy.

trying to get me in a corner. (Nobody puts Lola in a corner!) Anyway, I get the feeling Lexy doesn't want to share her things with me because she doesn't like it when I go near her scratching board or her favorite hiding spaces.

But do you know what she did? She went into my suite and ate some of my food! The nerve! I didn't see her, but Mommy saw her coming out licking her lips so she knew what she was up to. I guess it's OK ,though, because I ate some of hers (and she actually didn't try to eat me for doing it!)! Things were going pretty good until Lexy actually did get me in a corner and we started swatting at each other. Mommy separated us, but we started again so it's back to "you know where" for me for the rest of the night. The good news is that I was out for 2 1/2 hours this time. I think this is a step in the right diretion. What do you think?

January 26, 2011

Today the roles were reversed. Yesterday Lexy was hard to win over, but today I have to admit it's me. I'm doing the most hissing and I'm swatting first and even running after Lexy. Mommy says it sounds like there are a bunch of snakes in the house! She also says she's proud of Lexy today because she's walking away from me most of the time. I think it's going pretty well though. Guess what I did? I went into Lexy's favorite box. Mommy said I'm a rascal. Well, she ate my food again so she deserves it. Mommy said I better eat up all my food or there's a chance Lexy'll eat a lot of it (I hear she likes to eat), especially my dry food.

Good news though! Mommy said that unless something goes terribly wrong, I can stay out all night! Her early morning meeting was cancelled so she can pay attention to us during the night if need be. Woo Hoo! Yes!

One of the best parts of the day is that I finally got to relax and stretch out on the couch. When I was facing Death Row I never thought this dream would come true. Life is good.

Stretching out on the couch, relaxed and happy.

January 27, 2011

I'm not being very nice to Lexy. She's trying to be my friend, rolling over and showing me her belly, and trying to sniff me because she's curious about me. But when she comes near me, I growl and hiss and swat at her and I even bother her when she's eating. I'm showing her she can't boss me around, that's for sure. I follow her around the house to bother her, but she walks away from me. Lexy often tries to come up to me to check me out, but I chase her away lickety split. I even cornered her in the bathroom once and Mommy had to come get her out.

Mommy told me Lexy is trying to be nice to me, but I'm just not ready to be her friend yet. I went through a big traumatic life event with being thrown away, going to the shelter and almost not making it out. (The drama continues because Lexy just came into the bathroom and started swatting me. Gee...some cats are so unpredictable. Maybe Mommy wasn't so right after all! She closed the bathroom door to give us all a break for a few minutes.)

January 28, 2011

This morning when Mommy called Lexy to eat, I knew what she meant and I followed them right into the kitchen. I started to eat Lexy's food and wouldn't let her eat so Mommy had to pull me away from her dish. She said she can't believe how bossy I can be. Well, if I'm going to be in charge around here, Lexy should get used to it now.

January 29, 2011

News, news, and more news! Where do I begin? Well, last night Mommy had me back "you know where", because she wasn't sure what would go on during the night and she had to get up early for school. Turns out I woke her up VERY early, at 5:00 a.m., meowing and scratching at the door to get O-U-T! She let me out for a while in the morning, but put me back in when she left. Will came by to babysit and let me out.

And guess what I did? I sniffed noses with Lexy! Mommy was in class and missed it, but Will sent her a text message which I will quote: Ahem..."Lexy and Lola sniffed each other without incident." Yay! It was the only time we got close, but it's a start for sure. When Mommy got home she was very happy to see things were quiet, so she opened the bedroom door, which has usually been off limits when I've been out until now. She declared, "Time to get used to the whole house!" Then she started cleaning the bathroom (which I didn't like so much). She said she couldn't believe she was hearing herself say she was actually happy to get in there and clean. She tore the whole room apart and got out the vacuum and the steam mop. I didn't like what was going on and hid under the bed. Too much commotion and noise, and she moved my stuff around! She left my litter box in there though, which is good. And my food is in there for now, too.

When she was done she coaxed me out from under the bed, but I ran from her. She caught me and brought me to the couch to sit on her lap, which made me feel better. I even meowed at Lexy, but she was lounging on her favorite chair and didn't come play with me. So I found a toy and started playing by myself. I don't play for very long, but Mommy says it's good that I'm starting to show interest in things.

The best news is that I'm out for good! I've already been told that there will be no hissing on the bed tonight! Lexy likes to sleep on the bed, and we all have to live in peace and harmony in this apartment. Mommy said "maybe" I will go into the suite when she goes to work on Monday, but it all depends on what happens tomorrow. I think I can do it!

January 31, 2011

Lexy is really being a good sport. She's very playful and she's just dying to get me to play with her. She squats down and wiggles her butt and then runs toward me. I always get scared and hiss and growl and put my ears back. She doesn't know what to make of this situation and just walks away (unless I start swatting at her). I think her feelings are hurt. I can't help it; I'm still scared to death sometimes.

Like today, when Mommy came home I went into the kitchen to eat, but when she started putting pots away I ran for the hills! She brought my food into the bathroom (I call it the bathroom now since I don't live there anymore), but I kept running from her and hiding. I even ran and hid under the bed. Lexy followed me, but Mommy shooed her away because she knew I'd be scared. Now I'm playing a little bit with a toy I like, but I still run at the slightest noise. It seems I'm a little more scared now than I was before. Maybe it's because I'm not used to having so much room during the day. First I was in the cage, then I lived in the bathroom, and now I live in the whole house. I feel safe in the bathroom but then I meow and scratch at the door to get out. What's a girl to do?

I do have good news to share today: Lexy and I spent the whole day alone. When Mommy came home, Lexy was sleeping on the bench by the door and I was on the towel rack...

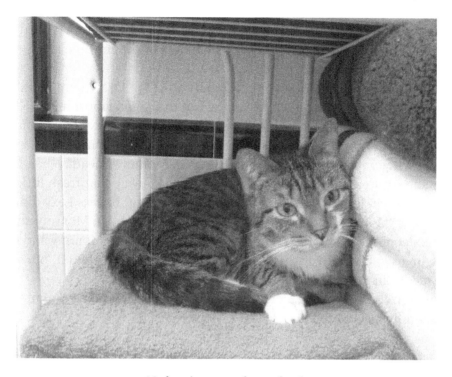

My favorite spot on the towel rack.

...and the house wasn't torn apart. That's good, right?!

February 1, 2011

This morning I was told I should be sure to eat all of my food, because if I don't Lexy will most likely eat it. Then Mommy will have two problems:

1. Lexy will get too heavy (and she looks like she put on a few ounces. Don't tell her I said that!) And,

2. I'll still be too skinny. She wants me to weigh eight pounds. Eight pounds? That's a lot! I only weigh about 5 pounds now.

February 2, 2011

I am the smartest cat I know. Mommy always says "Lexy is so smart. She's the smartest cat I've ever had." Pfffttttt, she's got nothing on me. Mommy taught Lexy what "Do you wanna eat?" means. Whenever she says it, Lexy gets all excited, her eyes get real big, and she runs behind Mommy into the kitchen. If Mommy is in the kitchen and yells

"Do you wanna eat?" Lexy comes running like a racehorse. Well, I didn't need anyone to teach me what that means. I know when it's breakfast or dinner time and I go into the kitchen all by myself. How smart is that?

If Lexy doesn't wake Mommy up, Mommy will say "Come here, Lexy!" and she goes running into the bedroom and hops on the bed to say good morning. Well, I figured that out all by myself, too. This morning when Mommy called Lexy I went into the bedroom, too, to join the party, but I guess I wasn't invited. You should have seen the look on Lexy's face when I was sitting on the pillow next to Mommy's head! When I went over to sniff her she swatted at me, and when I went to walk away that fresh little cat swatted at my butt! But at least there was no hissing or growling. I guess Lexy didn't like me intruding on her "Mommy and me time." That's OK, I get my own Mommy and me time when Lexy is sleeping on the chair and I jump on the couch with Mommy and I just purr, purr, purr. Anyway, I tried to go up to Lexy and sniff her again later on, but she backed away from me. I can't win.

Tonight we're not getting along so well. Maybe Lexy is still mad at me about this morning. Mommy just doesn't know what to do with us!

February 3, 2011

Guess what? Mommy and Will took me to see Dr. Plotnick today and everyone was so happy to see me! They couldn't believe how good I look! EVERYODY came in to say hello to me! I'm still a little sneezy and my eyes are a little runny, but Dr. P said I'm doing just fine. And I now weigh 5 pounds 12 ounces! I have to go back in a month for a test and then in six months for a follow up. I'm doing good!

February 4, 2011

This afternoon Mommy had to go to the store, and when she left I was sleeping in the bed next to Will when he was taking a nap. She was happy to see this, because I NEVER sleep on the bed. When she came home Lexy was in my spot and I was under the bed. Will didn't see anything because he was sleeping and Mommy laughed because she thought it was funny. (I wouldn't tell her what happened, though. I'm not going be a tattletale.) Later on she came to look for me to see what I was up to, and this is where she found me:

Lexy saw me there too and came to check the situation out, but I scared her away. I was told I am going to have to share the bed, because Lexy has taken it over since last April when she came to live here. I'm working on my sharing skills.

February 5, 2011

I'm just too cute for words, if I do say so myself. This morning

Sneaking a nap in Lexy's spot on the bed.

when Mommy was in the shower, she heard me meowing and meowing. When she came out, she saw me running around with the toy mouse in my mouth just meowing away! I was throwing it up in the air and catching it, too. Mommy said I looked like I was look-

Playing with my mouse for the first time.

ing for a place to hide it. She was able to snap this photo of me holding my mouse (well, technically it's Lexy's mouse, but I like to hog all the toys).

When I went to finish my breakfast I took the mouse with me and laid it down next to my bowl while I ate. Mommy said that now that I have a nice home, I'm finally living the kittenhood I never had.

21

February 6, 2011

Miracles always happen! Lexy and I were on the bed at the same time and she came over and sniffed me! She jumped off the bed after that, but at least she didn't try to beat me up. And guess what I did this morning? I woke Mommy up just like Lexy does, and I beat Lexy to it! Although Mommy was happy to see me she wasn't thrilled about being waken up at 6:45 on Sunday because this is the only day she can sleep late. Humans are so fussy about their sleep.

February 8, 2011

Last night I made the mistake of chasing Lexy away from me. I chased her all the way into the kitchen and now she thinks I want to play. All she did last night is chase me around the house. She would squat down, wiggle her butt, and CHARGE! It scares the heck out of me! So I start hissing or growling and try to hit her. This morning as I walked by her she rolled over on her back and showed me her belly and did the "kitty inching" toward me and tried to touch me with her paw. But I hit her, so she hit me back. The more I run from her, the more she runs after me, and then we get into it. Mommy tried to explain that she wants to play and that's how cats play with each other, but I never had a cat to play with so I don't like it. At least Lexy is being nice to me now. I guess that's what having a big sister is all about.

February 11, 2011

Boy, did I surprise Mommy tonight! Let me set the scene for you: On a usual night when she comes home, Lexy is usually at the door and she either pokes her head out or tries to open the door with her paw. (And sometimes she tries to make a run for it.) I run and hide behind the wall unit because I don't know who's coming in. Well, tonight when Mommy opened the door out popped Lexy's head as usual. Mommy shooed her back inside and bent down to pick up her groceries, and then all of a sudden out popped another little head. It was me! I met Mommy at the door for the first time! And for the first time I was curious about what was on the other side of the door. Mommy is proud of my progress. Now if she could only get Lexy to stop eating my food—she had to shoo her away from my bowl twice already since she's been home.

One more piece of news. Today for the first time, Mommy left the bedroom door open when she went to work. I was lying on the bed and she said I just looked too comfy to disturb. Both Lexy and I were in one piece when she got home, so she said she'll leave it open all the time now. Things are getting better!

February 12, 2011

Mommy really loves me. She washed towels, which usually means she fills the towel rack. But because she knows that's my favorite place, she is leaving half of it empty just for me! That's my safe place and I like to sleep there at night. This is really home.

February 16, 2011

Guess what? One month ago today I came to my new home! Today already started out great. Lexy didn't mind me sitting on the bed this morning with her and Mommy, and we even sniffed noses a couple of times. I can't believe how far I've come in a month. Thank you, Aunt Leslie, for being my guardian angel and saving me from the shelter.

February 17, 2011

I have the biggest news ever today! Guess where I slept last night? On the couch? Nope! On the recliner? Nope. On my pink towel? Nope! I slept on the bed with Mommy AND Lexy! Can you believe it? Lexy slept on the foot of the bed where she always sleeps (I don't know why, because she gets kicked from time to time, but she likes it there), and I slept up top, and she didn't even chase me away. Lexy left sometime during the night, but I stayed there until morning. It was very, very comfy. I can't wait for Will to see me sleeping on the bed when Lexy is there; he's going to be so surprised. Oh, and I stole Mommy's pillow from her. Well, she said I had to learn to share the bed with Lexy, so she'll have to share her pillow with me.

February 18, 2011

I had company today! Aunt Leslie came to visit me. Oh boy, did I get hugs and snuggles and kisses! We had such a lovely visit and I hope she comes to see me again soon.

February 20, 2011

Today's news: I ate most of my dinner in the kitchen, which is a big step for me. I get startled when there is noise, but Mommy stayed quiet and I ate a lot of it there. I'm also starting to watch Mommy do things more. Tonight I watched her wash the dishes. And yesterday I sat in the windowsill and watched the birds. So many things to see!

February 21, 2011

I love carrying my mouse all over the house. I always lie on the couch with it. Brown Mousie is my best friend. (If you look closely, you can see that I don't really tuck my paws. I kinda cross my arms in front of me. Mommy thinks it's cute.)

My best friend and me.

February 24, 2011

I have 171 friends on Facebook! When I was sitting in that dumpster, and then the shelter, I felt so alone. When I got to the hospital I started making friends, but I never thought I'd have this many! My wish is for all animals to feel this kind of love.

February 28, 2011

Boy, did I get in trouble last night. I posted a picture on my Facebook page of Lexy sniffing my nose. All my friends were so happy about the picture that I didn't even want to tell what happened after that. But Mommy said I have to be honest with my friends.

Well, Lexy jumped on the bed to sniff noses with me, which Mommy said was very sweet. As everyone saw in the picture I was very nice. Later on, Mommy was calling me to dinner and I didn't come so she started looking for me. She looked, and looked, and then out of the corner of her eye she saw me lying on Lexy's chair in her favorite spot.

She said "Hmmm" to herself, but let me stay there. When Lexy jumped up to check out the situation, I hissed at her and started hitting her. Mommy was not happy.

Later on I walked right up to Lexy and started sniffing her. She went to give me a kitty kiss and I got on my hind legs and hissed and started hitting her and fur started flying. Again, Mommy wasn't happy. Let's just say I got a stern speaking to. Mommy said Lexy opened up her heart and her home to me and she would like me to be nicer. She's wondering what goes on when she's not home. Oh no! I hope that doesn't mean going back to the bathroom!

I hope Lexy doesn't find me in her favorite spot!

Sigh. I'm trying, I'm really trying.

March 2, 2011

Stop the presses! I'm putting out an All-Points Bulletin on my mousie! It is nowhere to be found! Mommy looked, and Will even looked with a flashlight. No luck. Will bought me a new one, but it's not the same because this is the first toy I ever really had. If you happen to see my mousie, please hold it for me so I can come pick it up? Thank you.

March 2, 2011

Oh happy day! Mommy found my mousie! It seems I brought it onto her bed and it got stuck between the box spring and the headboard. I've been running around, throwing it up in the air, and meowing my little head off since I got it back! Mommy even got some video. Yay! I feel so much better now.

March 5, 2011

Although Lexy and I had a bit of a misunderstanding yesterday, she still slept on the bed with me for a while last night. I should say "us," since Mommy was there, too. Lexy still sleeps way down at the bottom and faces away from me, but she was there. I think she came in because Mommy told her she misses her on the bed at night. It was peaceful sleeping!

We found Mousie!

Settling In

March 6, 2011

I have a new thing! When Mommy is on the computer, I like to jump on her lap. She says if I would just sit on her lap and stay there that would be OK. But I climb all over her and she can't see what she's doing.

I'm much more interesting than the computer, Mommy.

When she's very busy, she sits too close to the keyboard so I can't get up there. I said to myself, "I don't like this one bit!" So I thought about it...

Thinking about how to get Mommy's attention.

...and thought about it...

I have a plan.

...and finally I solved my problem. I don't jump onto her lap anymore; I jump onto the back of her shoulders from the floor! It's really cool! And from up there I can get to even better places! Like here:

Wow! I can see everything from up here!

There are so many new things to see from up here! And Lexy has never even been up here. I did something before she did! I like it up here and I even gave myself a bath while relaxing in my new spot. I don't know how happy Mommy is about me being up here, but she thinks I can only get up there if I jump on her shoulders first. Hmmm, we'll see, won't we?

March 7, 2011

Brown Mousie is missing again. But don't panic! Big Black Mouse is here. It's still not the same as Brown Mousie, at least he's here to keep me company and help me practice my hunting skills. Mommy found Big Black Mouse in the bed this morning and she said it's a good thing she saw him or he'd be missing, too!

March 8, 2011

This morning Lexy and I started running around chasing each other and making noise. It was very early. Mommy got out of bed and informed us that she doesn't get up at 5:30 a.m., that when the alarm goes off at 5:10 it's for Will, not for her and us. Well, we didn't listen and kept making a racket. She came back out and said she was trying to sleep and said "so is the man who lives downstairs." She took me in the bedroom and closed the door, but it wasn't closed very tight so Lexy got in (she's a smart one, that Lexy) and set me free! She came out and picked me up again and put me on the bed, but I didn't want to stay. So she started petting me and once I started purring she knew she had me. I cuddled up next to her and we both went to sleep. When she turned over I thought it was time to get up and started meowing, so she played that trick on me again and started petting me. I started purring, and she had me again. This time I put my head next to hers on the pillow and my paw on her shoulder, and we took a little nap.

Now, Lexy knows Mommy's EVERY move. She knows her schedule better than Mommy even knows it herself. So I'm going to have a talk with her and ask why she didn't tell me 5:30 is too early to be making noise. I need Lexy to tell me everything I'm supposed to know.

Lexy and I usually watch Mommy get ready in the morning, but today we didn't. We were both too tired from getting up so early. Kitties need their beauty sleep, you know.

March 9, 2011

News of the day: the towel rack is now a towel rack again. Since I don't use it anymore, Mommy said she would put the towels back on it. I don't think I need it anymore. I have the bed and the couch, and the bench by the door, and the chair, and even Lexy's chair! I even have a bed, but I don't use that either. The furniture is better!

March 10, 2011

I heard Mommy tell Will that she has to go away for work for a few days. At first I got nervous because who is going to feed us and play with us? She said Will is going to check on us at night, and best of all Aunt Leslie is coming to take care of us! EXCITING!

Lexy is super happy because she won't have to go sleep in a cage at the vet. It reminds her of the shelter and she gets scared. (My poor sister). Mommy is noticing that I'm not eating as much as I usually do and that I sound a little more congested than usual. She's keeping an eye on it.

March 11, 2011

Update: I ate my food overnight (just about all of it anyway) and this morning I'm playing with my mousie and running from Lexy. No sneezes yet this morning, but I sneeze every single day so sneezes are normal for me. I'm sneezy, what can I say? Last night Mommy said she can hear me coming with this stuffy nose, but so far this morning I can sneak up on her. I'm due for a checkup anyway, so she has to make an appointment.

March 13, 2011

I tried to get out of going to the doctor tomorrow, but they called to confirm my appointment and Mommy said "We'll be there." She said if I had eaten my breakfast maybe she would have put it off. Stupid breakfast.

March 14, 2011

I went to see Dr. P today. Let me tell you, I do not like to leave the house—at all! I meowed all the way there and all the way home. And the big city has a lot of big scary noises that I don't like either. But anyway, here's the scoop. Dr. P gave me some antibiotics and L-lysine paste to take for ten days. He said I probably have a little bit of a cold and if I don't start eating more in the next few days I have to go back. In the meantime, he told Mommy to give me "smelly" food so I can smell what I'm eating. She bought me some tuna fish for dinner, and as you know, that can be smelly.

But there is some good news, too. I weigh 7 pounds 5 ounces! And my feline immunodeficiency virus (FIV) test came back negative. Whew! But here's something interesting: Mommy thought I was a year old cause that's what my papers from the shelter say. But Dr. P told her he estimates my birthday to be June 2010 so that means I'm about 9 months old, not a year old. Mommy said, "Poor Baby! She was only six months old when someone put her in the dumpster?" You know, that was really mean, not nice at all. I was just a baby. And as sweet as I am, who could not want me? But now I have Mommy and Will and Lexy, and Aunt Leslie, too, so I have a good life now. And I also have all of my friends on Facebook!

I got a mani/pedi when I was in the office because Mommy said a girl's nails always need to look neat. And I scratch her when I climb on her. I don't think that's a big deal, but she says it hurts.

March 16, 2011

Lexy and I were partners today hunting a bug.

We make a good team!

Mommy was happy we were getting along so nicely. I hate to burst her bubble, but it was a one-time thing.

March 19, 2011

This morning when Mommy called us for breakfast, I didn't want to leave the window (even though I had a hard time looking out because the blinds were down; I can't open them like Lexy can.) So she brought my food to me and I ate a little, but I was more interested in the birds outside. She left ¼-cup dry food which was gone when she came home, but here's the question: Who ate it? Hmmm, who do you think? I'm running and jumping and playing and looking out the window and stealing Mommy's things off her dresser, so all in all I'm doing well. I'm still taking my medicines and still a little sneezier than usual, but I don't have a snotty nose, which is a good sign.

Mommy bought some different Fancy Feast appetizers to give us a special treat, and at first I didn't eat any of it. (Lexy didn't eat it either; she's a little picky about her food). So sneaky Mommy put some dry food on top of it and I ate it. It wasn't bad at all, but she tricked me. Actually, that trick was Will's idea—wait till I see him!

March 20, 2011

Brown Mousie is back! Will found him for me! Thank you, Will! Mommy said she never saw me so happy before. I really missed him. He's my best friend.

March 24, 2011

Boy, do I know how to train a human. I taught Mommy to sit with me while I eat and to take some of the food out of the bowl for me because I like to eat that way, too. And you know what else I taught her to do? If I'm sitting in the window, she'll bring my food to me to make sure I eat. And I'm eating for sure! This is the life.

March 25, 2011

I saw Aunt Leslie today! She came to visit us and get information from Mommy on what we like to eat and what we like to do. And I have more news: I ate by myself today and Mommy didn't have to sit with me or bring me my food. When she got home, I was looking for food in the kitchen. I guess I'm better now!

March 30, 2011

Mommy is home today. Yay! Lexy and I woke her up at 5:30 and she said that was too early on her day off. Well, I'm a cat, so I don't know how to tell when it's her day off. I would think humans would want to get up early to spend extra time with their kitties, just like I get up extra early to spend time with Mommy.

April 1, 2011

Mommy let me eat in the kitchen window again, but she forgot to go look to make sure I ate everything she put out. When she came back later I heard her say, "Those ants are here again!" I ran to look, but I didn't see Aunt Leslie, Aunt Tamar, or any of my other Aunties. I looked up at Mommy and gave her the silent meow because I didn't know what she was talking about. She looked at me and said, "No ants allowed!" Huh, does that mean Aunt Leslie can't come take care of me anymore? I went to find Lexy to ask her about this. Lexy told me ants are bugs and we're supposed to pounce on them and eat them. I asked, "So next time Aunt Leslie comes here, I'm supposed to pounce on her and eat her?" Lexy shook her head and mumbled, "What am I going to do with you, Little One?" and she went to scratch on her scratching post. I still don't know why my Aunts can't sit in the window if they want to. I don't get it.

April 2, 2011

Taking a cat nap on Mommy's lap.

Mommy sent me to spend the day with Will. We had to get a new toilet, and there were workers in and out of the house all day making noise. She thought I might be too frightened, plus she didn't know how Lexy and I would do in the bedroom together all day. Mommy said later that Lexy was scared! She kept hiding under the bed, she was so frightened. I had a good time with Will (I packed Brown Mousie so I could have a little bit of home with me), but it was good to get home. I missed my chair, and my sister, and the kitchen window. And Mommy, too, of course. I was so happy to see her that I took a little cat nap on her this evening.

P.S. I could tell Lexy was happy to see me, because she kept following me around while I licked the curtains and sniffed everything to make sure the house was OK.

April 6, 2011

What a rainy day, and Mommy has to work far away today. She has to go over a bridge to get there. I wish she could stay home, but she says her work keeps the crunchy food overflowing in my bowl. I guess I better let her go then. I smell her coffee brewing, so it must be breakfast time. Better go eat!

April 8, 2011

Lexy has a scratch on her nose. I plead the fifth! (The fifth of what I'm not sure, but I plead it.) Especially since Mommy is not pleased with the scratch.

April 9, 2011

Every morning, I wake Mommy up by rolling around on her pillow, rubbing her face, sitting on top of her, and purring. Sometimes Lexy comes in to wake up Mommy to feed her, and she'll jump on the night stand and give her nose kisses. This morning when Lexy jumped up on the night stand, I went over to say hello, and guess what she did? She started giving me nose kisses and then...wait for it... SHE LICKED ME! She was licking my little head! Mommy said, "See how sweet Lexy wants to be with you,

Lexy found my hiding spot.

Lola? No more scratching please." I gave her the silent meow, but it didn't work. She's on to me with that.

About that scratch; Lexy chases me and I get scared. I run into the wall unit and hide next to the VCR. Lexy starts trying to touch me so I hit her and hiss at her. But the good news is SHE LICKED ME!

April 10, 2011

You know what one of my favorite things is? Mommy's jewelry! I take it off of her dresser all the time, and I've lost one of her earrings and a necklace. I found the chain but not what goes on the chain. I love to play with jewelry, it's so pretty! And just to have fun I'll hide it on purpose and watch Mommy look for it.

April 11, 2011

I have a very important job every night, and that job is to protect Mommy! I stay on the bed all night and make sure she's OK and that nothing happens to her. I even bring Brown Mousie to keep me company. Sometimes I throw him up in the air and catch him, and sometimes I lie on my back and hold him in my paws and kick him. Mommy always looks to see what is going on. I tell her it's just me on my watch making sure she's OK. Sometimes I get down to get a snack or a drink and check out the rest of the house to make sure everything is safe. When Will is here, I try to wake him up in the middle of the night to see if he wants to help me on my watch, but he only hides his face and goes back to sleep. In the morning, he tells me he doesn't like to get up in the middle of the night. Gee, I guess it's a good thing they have me to watch over the house!

Last night I asked Lexy if she wanted to come help me with this very important job. She laughed, shook her head and said, "That's OK Little One, you stay there and keep Mother company and I'll stay out here where I have plenty of room and peace and quiet." Then she went into her igloo cube and shut her eyes.

Keep Mommy company?! Hmpff! The nerve of that Lexy! I don't keep Mommy company; I protect her and keep her safe, and that's a very important job. Lexy thinks she knows everything, the big show off. And you know what else I do that's important? I don't let Mommy sleep late and I always make sure she gets up early. Lexy should appreciate that, because if Mommy sleeps too late then Lexy will eat late. But I make sure she's up. (Will doesn't get up when I tell him to, though. I'm still working on him.) Not every cat can do the job that I do!

April 12, 2011

Advice for my furry friends: Don't sneeze in your human's face when you wake them up. They'll make you get off the bed.

April 13, 2011

Mommy weighed me tonight on the human scale, and even though she says it may not be accurate, she thinks I weigh at least eight pounds, maybe more. Eight whole pounds! OK, Mommy, NOW will you stop worrying about what I eat? I'm not too skinny anymore!

April 14, 2011

Yesterday Mommy only worked a half a day and then was at home for a while before she had to leave for school. Before she left, she said goodbye to Lexy and me and told me, "You ignored me all day, Lola." Huh? I was sleeping on my chair the whole time; what is she talking about? I figured her feelings were hurt, so I decided to make it up to her. This morning, at 4:30 a.m., I decided to pay attention to her. I started rubbing her face with mine and purring. (And I didn't even sneeze on her.) And you know what she did? She covered her face and said "Not now Lola, it's only 4:30 in the morning." Who cares what time it is? I was making her feelings better. So first she said I ignored her, and then she wouldn't pet me when I paid attention to her. What's a cat to do? I can't figure humans out. They go by the clock too much.

April 15, 2011

I'm such a trickster! I played a big trick on Mommy this morning. When she got in the shower, I started meowing, just a regular meow at first. She called out "Lola, where are you?" I giggled to myself because I had a plan. I then let out a bigger meow, sorta like this: MEEEOOOWWW. "Lola, come here, Lola." Hee hee hee, this was so funny. Then I really let out a meow. MRRRRROOOOOOOWWWW-WRRRRRRR! The loudest meow of my life. Mommy got out of the shower and called "Lola? Lola? What are you doing?" And then I laid down the punch line; I came running toward the bathroom with Brown Mousie in my mouth. I was only playing! Mommy said "Good Lord" and got back in the shower. I'm funny.

April 16, 2011

How to wake your human up early and not get yourself in trouble: Get another kitty in your house to chase you and make a whole lot of noise. The human will call you to get on the bed and stop making noise. Then you've got their attention. Mission accomplished.

April 17, 2011

Today is a very, very special day. One year ago today, Mommy went with Auntie Ruthie (she's my real aunt because she's Mommy's sister) to pick Lexy up from the pet store! Her adoption from the no-kill shelter was official. So now Lexy has been in her forever home for one whole year. Hooray for Lexy! Mommy said it took her a while to settle in because she wasn't used to being able to run free. Lexy had lived at the shelter for almost a whole year after she was abandoned. But soon enough Lexy became Queen and took over the apartment and decided to let Mommy live here with her. That was really nice of Lexy. Here's picture of Lexy on her first day at home:

Lexy on her first day at home.

Mommy said Lexy was so excited to look out of the window. I bet she didn't get a chance to do that a lot before she left the shelter.

Happy Anniversary, Lexy! And thank you for being a great big sister and letting me live here, too. And you should know Mommy always says bringing both of us home was the best things she ever did. (Lexy is such a great big sister that I made sure her rescue story is included at the end of this book!)

April 20, 2011

Lexy learned something from me! Imagine that! This morning when Mommy was in the shower she started meowing from the living room. She usually sits in the bathroom on the tub to watch the water, but today she didn't. Lexy is not a "meower" and she has a loud meow, so Mommy got nervous at first and started calling "Lexy? Lexy?" from the shower. We both started giggling in the living room. We're both tricksters now.

April 21, 2011

Mommy is baking, and I don't like it one bit. Too many noises and smells coming from the kitchen and it's hot in there. I keep poking my head around the corner to check on the situation. But you know what Mommy did? She brought my food and water to the bathroom for me. How lucky am I? I'm glad Mommy understands me.

April 22, 2011

Lexy went to the vet today to get chipped and clipped. Wow, that sounds scary! The vet is a very traumatic experience for her, so I decided to be nice for once. When she got home, I was waiting for her at the door, and I think she appreciated it! Mommy says a little bit of nice goes a long way. I think she's right!

April 23, 2011

Mommy is baking AGAIN! Soon there will be a holiday called Easter, and Lexy told me Mommy likes to bake for holidays. What's all this fuss about "fresh baked goods"? How much stuff can humans eat? Can't you all just be happy with a small bowl of crunchy stuff like me? Lexy loves to watch her and is sitting on the kitchen chair keeping her company. Too much noise for me. Will is watching TV in the bedroom, so I'll just go keep him company.

April 26, 2011

Mommy looked at me today and commented, "Lola, you're getting tall!" She thinks when I'm all done growing and gaining weight that I'll be bigger than Lexy. Then I'LL be the big sister. Let's see how Lexy likes that!

April 28, 2011

Mommy tried to wake me up by rubbing my face. I wasn't impressed with her cat impersonation. If she licked my nose, though...

April 29, 2011

I played another trick on Mommy this morning. (What else is new?) She felt something moving under the covers and muttered, "What the heck is that?" When she looked, she found little old me. I made a tunnel under the covers and was running around down there. Mommy didn't think 4:00 a.m. was a good time to play Secret Tunnel, so I jumped off the bed and started running around and scratching things. (I've been copying Lexy and scratching the box spring. That doesn't go over well.) She didn't think 4:00 a.m. was a good time for that, either. She said "Lola, you never had the night crazies. This is not a time to start." She called me back on the bed and I took my position as Protector. When I really wanted her to wake up, I tried something new. I usually rub her face, knead, and purr on top of her, and today I added a new twist: I licked her nose! That got her attention! I hope I'm not running out of ideas. I may have to do a Google search to find new things to do.

May 1, 2011

Mommy went to the doctor today, and she has surgery scheduled for her hand next month. Lexy said she had her other hand done a few months before I moved in and she was fine. Lexy said not to worry and we'll be able to take good care of her. She'll be home for a long time and that will be fun. What would I do without Mommy, though? I guess Will would take care of us, but I'd hate to end up with no home again. And I would miss her terribly.

May 6, 2011

Humans get too crazy over a little bit of cat hair. I hardly ever lie on the bed in the morning because I'm just way too busy. I'm usually enjoying the breeze in the kitchen window, taking a bath in the sun, or watching the leaves blow and looking for the birdies. I also have to ask Mommy to bring me my food to the window. That's a lot of work! This morning I wasn't in my usual place, so Mommy went looking for me and lo and behold, she found me. Not only was I lying on the bed, but I was also lying on her pants, which she wasn't too happy about. What's a little bit of cat hair? I thought she'd like a little reminder of me all day. But out came the lint roller and away went the hair. Humans.

May 7, 2011

Mommy got excited today. Lexy was paying so much attention to her, purring, and getting petted. And today is Mommy's birthday so she was even happier to get this present. Then she realized Lexy was hungry and wanted to eat. My sister is something else.

May 9, 2011

Whenever Mommy leaves the house, she looks for us first to make sure we're not up to something and to make sure we didn't get locked in a closet. This morning she saw me in the kitchen, but couldn't find Lexy. When she walked back into the kitchen she found us together in the window.

A sisterly moment in the kitchen window.

41

She left saying how happy she is that we're friends now. I didn't have the heart to burst her bubble and tell her it was a moment of weakness, so I let her be happy—for now.

May 15, 2011

Exciting news! I met Mommy's friend Melissa for the first time today, and she loved me! (What's not to love?) She's a huge Lexy fan, so I did my best to make a good impression. When she came in I ran and hid under the bed because I still don't like strangers. But after a few minutes I came out and I let her pet me, and I even gave her lots of purrs and rubbed her face. I have a new friend!

May 18, 2011

There are so many stories of animal abuse and cruelty lately, and it's just terrible. Mommy is following two stories right now that she told us about. A kitty in England was abused by a man who did horrible things to her. That's a mean, mean, man. And then in Michigan someone shot a cat in the face and neck with an arrow! How horrible! *wipes tears with paws* I was lucky compared to these kitties and I'm so sad for them.

I found him! My best friend is back.

May 19, 2011

I'm starting a trend on Facebook. Cats are buying brown mousies just like mine! I think a big company should make "The Lola Brown Mousie" since I'm doing a lot of promotion. By the way, he's lost—again.

May 22, 2011

He's back! Brown Mousie is back! I'm so happy I don't know what to do with myself.

May 23, 2011

Some of my Facebook friends have been asking about my sneezes. I made sure they know I'm OK, that I don't have a cold or anything. I had to explain that my immune system isn't that strong and ever since I got that bad cold in the shelter, I'm sneezy. I'm just a sneezy cat now with a runny nose sometimes. Mommy always says "God bless you" when I sneeze, and goes to get a tissue to clean up the mess. No one has to worry, I'm in good hands.

May 24, 2011

Today is clean sheet day and I'm ready to supervise!

I don't know how Mommy survived without my help before I came to live here.

May 26, 2011

Lexy looked a little under the weather this morning. She threw up a big hair ball and then was following Mommy around everywhere. I think she's better now, because she ate her breakfast. My poor sister; I worry when someone in my family is sick.

May 27, 2011

Mommy was not a happy human last night. It all started around 2:00 a.m. Mommy heard a noise in the bedroom and

I'm supervising clean sheet day!

looked down to see where I was on the bed. I wasn't there. Then she saw me checking out the pile of stuff she has to bring to storage. This is very different for me, because I don't usually roam around the house at 2:00 a.m—I'm usually stretched out next to her, getting my beauty sleep. And then it started: Lexy and I started making lots of noise. Running around the bedroom, walking on the dressers, scratching at the bed, meowing—you know, doing cat stuff! Mommy tried and tried, but she finally caught me and tried to get me to come back to bed. Well, the bigger I get the harder it is to get me to do that, so I kept jumping off and playing. I finally decided to go back to bed and Mommy was very happy—until I started licking her nose and not letting her sleep. I finally decided to settle down a bit, but then Mommy heard a strange noise. She looked at me and I was lying very quietly. She looked around the room in the dark and saw Lexy near the bed, hunched over. At first she thought she was sick, but then she heard her rustling something around. Mommy turned on the light and you'll never guess what Lexy had! A package of chicken treats that she took from the cabinet! (Lexy can open the cabinet all by herself.) Mommy picked it up to put it back, but Lexy bit holes in it and it started leaking. What a mess. She said "Lexy, you don't even like these!" Mommy went into the kitchen and Lexy followed her, and I followed Lexy because I didn't want to miss out on anything. Mommy saw me and said, "You, too?" Mommy was so tired she just opened it and put it in a bowl and went back to sleep. Not too long later she heard a "PLOP." She looked and there was Lexy. She turned on the light and Lexy had ANOTHER packet! What a funny sister I have. Mommy said that was it and moved the treats to the closet. Everything finally quieted down when the birds started singing.

In the morning, Lexy had eaten some of the chicken, but left the big chunks of stuff that's in it. She doesn't like chunky things. And today Mommy put all the cat things that Lexy could possibly take in a plastic shoe box. I don't think Lexy will be opening that up. Or will she?

May 30, 2011

I have a new thing: I lie/sleep on the floor. I never did that before, but it's hot now and it's so much cooler down there. Mommy has to be careful because now she never knows where she'll find me. Oh, and she found a sneeze accident on the window. Oops. What can I say?

May 31, 2011

Lexy and I caught a bug together today. Now that's team work. Mommy always knows when I'm up to something because I meow and meow and meow. Lexy doesn't meow; she keeps things secret. And then she pounces! She's a really good hunter; I could probably learn a thing or two from her. I asked her if she ever lived on the street because she is such a good hunter, but Lexy won't meow much about her past to me. Mommy wouldn't let us eat the bug, which I didn't think was very nice after all that hard work.

June 1, 2011

I was sniffing Mommy's coffee this morning and she grabbed it away really fast! She said she didn't want a sneeze accident in her coffee. I don't think that would be such a big deal. I wouldn't mind if she sneezed in my food.

June 3, 2011

Mommy is having the operation on her hand tomorrow. I'm worried about her. Without Mommy there wouldn't be anyone to feed us or open the blinds. And there would be no one to give face rubs to and no one to pet us or love us. I'm going to take very good care of her, just like she took such good care of me when I was sick.

June 4, 2011

Mommy had her hand fixed and she's ok. I took very good care of her.

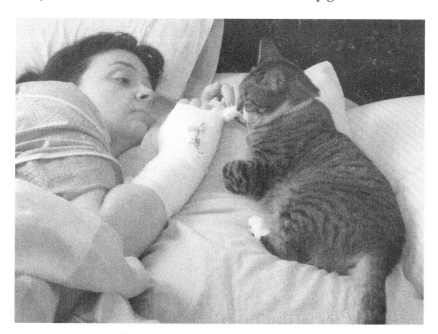

Taking care of Mommy, I'm the best nurse ever.

I'm so glad I'm here for her.

And this morning she surprised me so much! You're not going to believe it. Her time clock is all messed up because of her medication, and she got out of bed before me this morning—when it was still dark out. She didn't want to wake Will up, because he works really late tonight so she got her Kindle and went into the living room. I heard her rustling around in the closet for a blanket and came to investigate. After she got me out of the closet, she lay down on the couch and started to read a little but then got sleepy. Lexy was watching her from her shoe box and I knew Mommy was in good paws, so I went back to bed with Will so he wouldn't be lonely. When I heard it was breakfast time, I came out and now I'm going to nap on my recliner that Mommy cleaned so nicely the other day. I need to get my hair on it again so it's perfect.

June 5, 2011

Today Mommy had the NERVE to say that if Lexy and I are going to follow her around to make sure she cleans the litter boxes to our liking, then we'll have to scoop our own poop! Imagine that! First of all, I'm not scooping Lexy's poop, and second, I don't have thumbs. How can I scoop with no thumbs? And if Mommy did it right in the first place we wouldn't have to check up on her. Sometimes humans are so hard to teach.

June 7, 2011

I played a trick on Will last night! I was meowing my head off and he said to mommy, "Is that Lola?" Then I meowed again and he asked, "Is she alright?" and leaned up in bed to see if he could see me. Mommy said "she's got her mouse." MROWW-WWW MMRRRROOOWWWW "Is she alright?" "Yes, she's fine. She has her mouse." MMROOORRRRTTT. Then he went to look for me and told mommy, "She has her mouse." Does my mommy know me or what?

June 8, 2011

I had a little bit of a traumatic day. My nails were very long and I was scratching Mommy because I'm always kneading biscuits on her. Will said that since he was here, they could take me to get a mani-pedi. I wasn't very happy about that. The place was only ten minutes away, but I carried on from the time I was put in the carrier till we got there. I was so pitiful that Mommy almost told Will to turn around and take me home, but she didn't. I even did a little tinkle in the carrier.When we got there, a very nice young man and woman took care of me, and the man told Mommy I have an ear infection. That's not good. I didn't like the ride home either, and I let them know about it.

When we finally got back home, Will cleaned me with some kitty wipes so I wouldn't smell like tinkle. He's very nice to me. The bad news is that I have to go to the vet tomorrow. Mommy can't get me to Dr. P in the big city because of her hand, so I'm going to Lexy's cat doctor. I told my Facebook friends I'll keep them posted, and I let them all know now I'm NOT going to like the car ride, even if Mommy did buy me a better carrier today.

June 9, 2011

Doctors, doctors, doctors! Well, today started out with a bit of a commotion. After Mommy got me in the carrier with one hand, she couldn't find her keys. After a while she had to let me out—and of course then she found her keys! So back in I had to go, which wasn't easy, let me tell you. But we did it.

I was a little better today than yesterday. Mommy bought a calming spray which is supposed to help calm kitties. (Mommy said that stuff better work because it cost an arm and a leg. She already only has one hand, so what is she going to do without an arm and a leg?) I also had a hard carrier today which is really hard to fight my way out of. When we finally got to the cat doctor we had to wait a bit, but I was a good girl. A resident cat even came over to say hello and was sniffing Mommy's face.

This was my first time at Lexy's doctor, and she is such a nice lady. You know what she said about me? She said I'm a great cat and I'm so sweet. I charmed her. It turns out I don't have an ear infection, but my ear lobe is irritated, and I have conjunctivitis and I

I weigh 9 pounds 4 ounces!

got medicine for both. The cat doctor wants Mommy to give me L-lysine twice a day now instead of once because we have to get my immune system stronger. This way I don't have to be on medication all the time and get colds and infections. I can do it; I can get stronger.

Mommy couldn't believe it when the cat doctor told her I weigh 9 pounds 4 ounces! She said she won't bother me so much about eating anymore because I'm eating enough to be healthy. It's about time! The cat doctor felt so bad for me when Mommy told her my story and is so happy that I have a good home now. She said, "This is a happy cat."

I took a nap with Mommy when we got home, and everything is back to normal. Now it's time for medicine. Yuck.

June 10, 2011

Mommy says I don't seem myself today. I don't like that medicine stuff and I don't like her holding me down. I'm tired of medicine and of being sick!

Mommy is going to get her hair done at her groomer today. I hope they don't tell her she has an ear infection so she ends up at the human doctors.

June 11, 2011

Mommy thought I looked a little glum today, so she surprised me. I was in the kitchen window and she came to get me to follow her into the bedroom. And guess what? It was clean sheet day! That cheered me up! Nothing that makes this kitty happier than clean sheet day.

June 13, 2011

My good Facebook friend, Calculus Q. Jones, wrote a poem about me!

> *Lola the Rescued Cat*
> *Lola the cat, nearly sent to the dump*
> *An angel of Harlem, in a real slump*
> *But with love pure and true*
> *She soon found rescue*
> *And now she is living like Trump.*

Isn't it just fantastic?

June 14, 2011

Lexy and I were not good hostesses this morning. Mommy's friend, Melissa, slept over, and this morning we carried on something terrible until Mommy got up to feed us. Then we went back to bed.

June 16, 2011

Mommy is having company tomorrow and is doing some cleaning. You know what that means—the Shark is coming out! Run Lexy, hide! I think she should just leave our furs all over the furniture; we're only going to put it there again.

June 17, 2011

Mommy wasn't very happy with Lexy this morning. Yesterday she bought rolls for lunch for her company and Lexy ripped open the bag and started eating one. She did that with English muffins once, too. Took a whole muffin right out of the package! Mommy better think of a way to hide that hole in the roll before someone makes a sandwich.

June 21, 2011

I'm becoming very independent! I remember when I couldn't get behind the blinds and I had to wait for Mommy to pull them up for me.

Well, look at this. One day Mommy was sitting on the couch and she saw something in the window. "What the heck is that?" she wondered. It was just little old me—behind the blinds!

Another day she saw something in the bedroom window, but it was just me again.

It's so nice now that I don't have to wait for someone to pull up the blinds to look out and watch the trees and the birdies.

I can't see outside. Can you open these for me?

I can see outside all by myself now.

It's just me, Mommy. Don't worry.

I don't have to wait for someone to pull up the blinds anymore! It's so nice to look out and watch the trees and the birdies.

June 22, 2011

I can't figure out why Lexy likes boxes so much. She looks ridiculous! But I won't be the one to tell her.

June 23, 2011

I just took my last dose of eye ointment. I survived the treatment. I don't know if I can say the same thing about Mommy and her hand, though.

Why does Lexy like boxes so much?

June 26, 2011

Holy Cat! We had the biggest fly in the universe in the house. I hunted that thing for the longest time. Mommy tried to get it with the spray, but that didn't work and then she had to clean the window. Lexy came and caught it and had it in her mouth but Mommy wouldn't let her eat it. I tired the fly out so she could catch it. It's a good thing for Lexy I worked so hard.

Mommy and Will are leaving for vacation tomorrow, and Aunt Leslie will be coming to take care of us! They're going to a fishy place called Cape Cod. I hope they bring lots of cod home with them.

June 27, 2011

Today is a special day. It's my birthday celebration day and I am ONE YEAR OLD! I can't thank my Aunt Leslie enough for saving me and Mommy for giving me a good home. Six months ago I was lying in a cage with no family, and today I'm celebrating a birthday in my home. I'm so happy, I feel like crying tears of happiness. My wish is for all animals to be as lucky as I am.

June 30, 2011

Mommy being on vacation is cramping my style. I have tons of new friends on Facebook and I can't post. When will she learn my social life is more important than going away? I think vacations are stupid, anyway. Why would a human want to go away when they have all they need at home with their kitties?

July 1, 2011

Lexy is finally friends with Aunt Leslie! Look what she posted on her Facebook page today: "Lexy is my new BFF! Oh My Cat! She has been so shy with me in the past but this time, she follows me around, sniffs my mouth and eyes (love that!), and does sillies!" That's my sister! It takes her time to come around to humans that aren't Mommy or Will. She doesn't trust very easily.

July 3, 2011

Mommy is home! I hid under the bed at first and wouldn't come out, but then I sniffed and realized it was her. I'm going to miss Aunt Leslie, though. I'm hoping she comes to visit me, especially since she and Lexy are besties now. Thank you, Aunt Leslie, for taking such great care of us.

Hard at work helping Mommy fold the sheets.

July 5, 2011

Mommy was cleaning closets today and it was a lot of hard work. It's a good thing I was here to help her.

July 6, 2011

Today something very, very terrible happened. A kitten was thrown out of a car on the Verrazano Bridge. I just don't understand why a human would do something so mean to a kitty! They can just find the kitty a new home, can't they? Even if they have to take it to a shelter, it's better than being mean and hurting it. Luckily the little kitty survived and is OK. This reminds me of being thrown in the dumpster. *trembles* I think I need to go snuggle with Mommy.

July 7, 2011

Tonight I jumped onto Mommy's lap when she was on the computer and sat on the keyboard shelf. She told me, "Lola, get your butt off the keyboard, please." So I did, and then I jumped on her and was rolling around and sitting on her chest. She said, "You know Lola; you don't weigh four pounds anymore." I know. I'm nine pounds! But I will always be her little kitty and will jump and roll on her. She's my Mommy and she has to put up with it.

July 8, 2011

Attention! (Is this thing on?) May I have your attention please! (tap tap tap). I have an official announcement to make. Ahem…I am now taller than Lexy. I AM TALLER THAN LEXY! Thank you for your attention.

July 12, 2011

Oh darn! Mommy said my eye was a little red again and it was leaking yucky stuff, so she started giving me that yucky eye ointment again. I've had enough of that stuff and my weak immune system that doesn't fight off germs. I wish I was as strong as Lexy.

July 15, 2011

Lexy went to get her mani-pedi today. She did well in the car and in the waiting room. But poor Lexy gets so scared in the exam room that she shakes and hisses non-stop. But guess what? She weighs 10.5 lbs. She gained 0.5 lbs. since November. That's because she eats my food!

July 17, 2011

I love the kitchen window. I love watching the birdies on the roof of the house next door.

I love the kitchen window.

July 20, 2011

My sister has to go to the vet tomorrow. Mommy noticed she has something on her mouth and it has to be checked. She's still eating my food, so it can't bother her that much.

July 21, 2011

Lexy's doctor said she has an allergic reaction to something and gave her a steroid shot. She's doing better already and that thingy isn't as swollen. Mommy has to watch and keep a log if it comes back. She said she has a swollen lip cat and a sneezy cat. What is she going to do with us?

July 22, 2011

I don't like Mommy going back to work. Today was the first time I got morning snuggles since she went back. It was the best belly rub I've gotten all week, and it's Friday! And you know what she forgot to do last night? She didn't scoop our litter boxes! That's terrible! And all she had to say about it this morning was, "Sorry, girls." There must be a law against this.

She put these little floaty things from the freezer in our water dishes this morning that she said would keep the water a little cool because it's hot out. But they disappeared after a few minutes, so I guess they didn't like it in there. And she left the big cold box on all day for us, "even though I'm going to owe Con Ed a mint." A mint is only a piece of candy so I don't understand why it's a big deal to owe Con Ed one. I got used to a lot more attention than this when she was home with her hurt hand. I think I'll have to tell her job she has to stay home more often. Kitties cannot be ignored. We have needs.

July 26, 2011

Mommy had the nerve to say my licking is getting a little out of hand. Can I help it if she doesn't like my tongue in her nose? I'm not stopping. I like it.

July 29, 2011

I am going back to the cat doctor. I was sneezing my head off last night and Mommy was up with me. Mommy tried to give me a steam in the bathroom tonight to help with my stuffy nose, but I didn't like it. Not one bit. The water was making noise and it was hot and steamy. I cried and cried to get out, and I wouldn't even sit on her lap. I don't like being locked up. Mommy is hoping one day I won't be so scared anymore.

July 30, 2011

I'm pretty cute when I'm sleeping, if I do say so myself.

I'm really cute when I'm sleeping.

August 1, 2011

Another trip to the cat doctor today. I wasn't getting in that carrier without a fight! Mommy thought she wasn't going to get me in at all. She kept saying, "Work with me here, Lola," "Lola, you're not working with me." Of course not; I didn't want to get in! But, I lost and ended up getting in. I don't like the carrier because it feels like a cage. After the dumpster and the shelter, I don't like being trapped in something.

But anyway, I tried and tried to get out, and kept sticking my little paws and legs through the front of the carrier. And I cried and cried the whole time I was in it. Mommy puts a big cushy towel in the carrier because I tinkle when I get nervous. Let's just say it's a good thing it was there. I carried on something terrible! The other kitties at the vet sat nicely, and one even sat on their owner's lap. Mommy wouldn't take me out no matter how much I asked. She didn't want me to try to run out the door.

In the exam room, though, I am a different cat. I'm such a sweetheart and everyone who meets me just loves me.

Since I don't do well in the car and the carrier, Mommy decided to stay close to home and take me back to Lexy's doctor. I gave the doctor a nose rub to charm her, but the charm didn't work because she said I have "a recurrence of the herpes virus" (those are fancy words to say I have a cold) and gave me medicine for ten days. She said it's nothing to worry about, and I'll probably get another one sometime in the future.

When we got home, Lexy ran to the door to see what was up and licked my head hello. She's a nice sister.

August 4, 2011

Guess what I did yesterday? According to Mommy, I "initiated play with Lexy." Mommy saw me crouching down and looking like I was on the hunt, but she didn't think anything of it. Sometimes I get the crazies and run around after nothing. But then Lexy walked by and I ran after her! I wasn't even mean to her. Then she chased me back and we ran around the house. Mommy was so happy. She probably shouldn't get her hopes up that this will be an everyday thing, because it won't be, but at least I made her happy.

August 5, 2011

Mommy's flip-flop makes a nice pillow. I think I may be onto something here. Maybe I can find an agent and sell flip-flop pillows. I'd be famous.

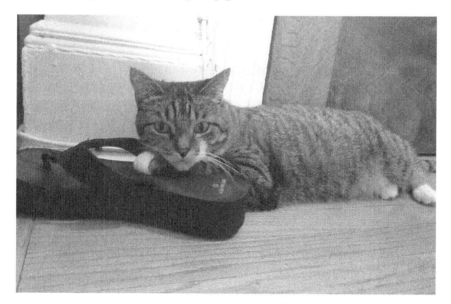

Mommy's flip flop is a nice pillow.

August 8, 2011

Trying to get cats saved is hard work! I've been posting my little paws off about kitties that need homes. A beautiful kitty is on the "list" (that means Death Row) because she has the sneezies. That's not a big deal, I had the sneezies and look at me today. My goal is to save the world, one rescued kitty at a time!

August 10, 2011

Last night I meowed my head off, louder than Mommy EVER heard me meow. I woke her right up out of her sleep! I was on the hunt and brought her my prize! I jumped on the bed and gave her my mousie. (Lucky for her it's not a real mousie—but THAT would be funny!)

August 12, 2011

Do you know it took me a whole hour and 15 minutes to wake Mommy up this morning? I started licking her nose at 5:15. When that didn't work, I walked on her and licked her again. She kept hiding her face so I licked her hands. I kept coming back and doing this until she finally got up at 6:30. By that time I was exhausted.

August 14, 2011

I have good news! Mommy says that since I finished this last round of antibiotics...ready to hear it? Wait for it...I HARDLY SNEEZE AT ALL ANYMORE! She's so happy, and so am I. She says I MUST take that L-lysine paste every day to keep herpes away, whoever he is. I guess my immune system is getting stronger!

Feeling Home At Last

August 15, 2011

Everybody knows how much I love Will. I love him with all my heart, and he's one of my best buddies. He's the only human I don't run from when he comes in the house. (Well, besides Mommy of course—depending on what kind of shoes she's wearing.) I even help him take his shoes off by chasing the shoelaces and watching them just to make sure they don't go anywhere and get lost. But there is one little problem....

When he isn't there, I have half of Mommy's bed all to myself. I stretch out right next to her with my head up top and my back paws down bottom, just like she does. Sometimes I lie on my back and put my little paws in the air. It's the best, and it's so cozy. It's my own side of the bed. But when Will is here, he sleeps on my side. It's MY SIDE! He is always nice and makes room for me, but I end up sleeping down on the bottom and get kicked around. I don't like it one bit.

So last night I took matters into my own paws and slept right on Mommy's pillow. And sometimes I could even stretch out onto Will's pillow at the same time. It was great! Mommy complained a little because she said she couldn't fit, and when she got up to use the bathroom I took over the whole pillow. She complained that she had a stiff neck and commented, "You know, you're not so tiny anymore." Well, she should have a bigger bed so I can stretch out and have my space. Or maybe Will should sleep in Lexy's igloo cube. Humans need to know kitties will not tolerate people taking over their space!

August 16, 2011

Mommy heard me meowing my "hunting meow" and looked to see which mousie I had. I didn't have a mousie; I had her necklace. I think I might be in trouble.

August 17, 2011

I think I'm in trouble again. Today Mommy came home and found her diamond earring on the floor in our little hallway. She can't figure out how I got it, and I'm not telling her.

August 22, 2011

Checking out my Facebook page.

Aunt Colleen and Shelby sent me a brown mousie that SQUEAKS!! Can you believe it? I posted a video of me playing with him on my Facebook page. Here I am checking it out. (This is what Mommy calls a "still" from it.) I need to see how many of my friends liked it.

August 27, 2011

Ms. Phoebe (AKA Mamma Pheebs, my Facebook friend) made me a Princess!

A Princess, complete with a crown!

I'm a Princess!

August 28, 2011

I was watching the news with Mommy, and it says Hurricane Irene is just about here and she sounds like she's really mad. Mommy got out our carriers, which I don't like. She also packed a bag with bowls, food, water, toys, leashes—and her toothbrush. I hope we don't have to leave. I'm saying a prayer for all the stray animals who don't have a warm, dry home and have to be out there in the storm.

August 30, 2011

Mommy got up so early for work today that I didn't even get out of bed when she got up. It was still dark outside! Even when she left, I was still in bed because it was just too early for breakfast in my breakfast nook in the kitchen window. (I need to make sure I get my beauty sleep.) Of course, Lexy got up. It doesn't matter what time Mommy wakes up; when she gets up, Lexy gets up and keeps her company.

September 5, 2011

I can't believe how lucky I am. Some of my friends made Lexy and me pretty pictures with words on them, and funny pictures of us, too. (Mommy says they're called graphics.) Now I will have an official Logo! Wow, this is exciting.

September 6, 2011

Tonight I walked over to Lexy and put my head down so she could lick it. I thought I'd do something to make Mommy happy. (Lexy needs a breath mint. This won't be happening again for a while.)

September 8, 2011

I should really be more appreciated around here. Mommy just doesn't seem to be grateful that I look out for her so much. This morning, I woke her up around 6:20, just like I've been doing all week. And what do I get? "Lola, I don't have to get up for another half hour." Well, then, how am I supposed to get my snuggles? And then when I kept licking her face and nose, she kept covering her head with the blanket. The nerve! But I didn't give up. "Lola, I have an alarm clock to wake me up. And you don't have a snooze button." Alarm clock? I think having one of my licks on the nose to wake you up is better than that noisy box. And I'm more cuddly than a box with numbers on it that makes a lot of noise.

I wouldn't let her snooze; I kept walking on her and sitting by her head purring, and I licked her until she finally got up. And Lexy was happy because she was hungry. I'm the best alarm clock Mommy could ever have. (And she better not get any ideas about a snooze button!)

September 11, 2011

I'm very sad today. My friend Shelby isn't doing well. Shelby is my Aunt Colleen's kitty and she's 18 years old. Another cat started a candle-lighting page to send light and love and prayers to Shelby. I just love how our cat community loves and helps each other through tough times. And if it wasn't for this community, I'd never have been adopted. It's very, very special.

September 13, 2011

Wow, I've been busy! I'm co-sponsoring a contest to get one of my Facebook friends, Pickles, more friends. Plus, I had an idea to put together two prize packages full of goodies to give to two of my oldest friends and followers on Facebook—people who have followed my story from the very beginning. I barely have time to meow at anyone these days.

September 16, 2011

You're never going to believe this: Mommy says she is trying to be a vegetarian. I cannot live with a cat doctor! If she thinks she's going to give me a shot in my butt, she better think twice!

September 20, 2011

Wow, I'm so smart, I surprise myself! I learned how to outsmart Mommy when she tries to give me my lysine paste. (That stuff tastes kind of yucky, and I don't like it when Mommy puts it in my mouth.) I didn't get it this morning! Let's just say it's a good thing she can't fit under the bed.

I'm Famous!

September 26, 2011

Oh my stars, you'll never believe the latest news. Sweet Pickles Designs named a collar after me. It's called The Lola!

My signature Sweet Pickles Collar—The Lola!

Modeling The Lola.

Now is that me, or what? It's all sparkly and looks like real jewels. I'm so flattered, I can't even meow about it. I'm so honored Pickles would do this.

I look gorgeous!

Another Rescue

September 28, 2011

Exciting news! Exciting news! I have a step-brother! Last Saturday Will saw a cat by his job, but then he never saw it again. Well, today the cat came back and came right up to Will! He noticed that the cat was skinnier than the last time he had seen it. This made him sad, so he went home and got his cat carrier and went back to work and took the kitty home. When Will got there, the kitty walked right up to him and started rubbing on him and got right in the carrier. Here is his picture:

Jack after being rescued.

He looks just like me, only he doesn't have white socks!

At first they thought it was a girl, so Mommy was calling it Lilly. (She thought a pretty girl should have an "L" name like Lexy and me.) But now they're pretty sure it's a boy, so they named him Jack.

Will says he doesn't really want another cat right now, because he still misses Tiger, who went to the Rainbow Bridge in November. But he says he'll take care of Jack as long as he has to. Tonight he went to look for a cat bed for him so he would be comfy. Mommy says that cat isn't going anywhere; she doesn't know who Will thinks he's kidding! Mommy would take him, but we can't have any more pets where we live.

On Sunday, Jack is going to the vet to see if he has a chip. Mommy says he came from a home because he's so friendly and sweet with people. He made himself comfy and lay right on Mommy's foot tonight! Now he's relaxing with Will on his couch. The security guard at Will's job told him that Jack would go out to the sidewalk and walk up to people. He's a people cat. So maybe Jack has a chip and he can go home to his family. It's great that another cat is off the streets. Thank you, Will.

September 30, 2011

Mommy bought me breath mints. I think I'm insulted. I don't tell her to go brush her teeth when she gets up in the morning; I love her just like she is. And let me tell you, there is nothing pleasant about morning breath.

October 1, 2011

Mommy caught me in the act this morning. The big mystery question is, what was I doing? Drum roll please...What Mommy caught me doing was...LICKING LEXY! I only let her see me do it for a second, but she caught me. She thinks I secretly like Lexy, but just won't let people know. Or Lexy either, for that matter.

October 2, 2011

Here's Jack's update: Jack was such a good boy in the carrier and at the vet. (Hmmm... Lexy and I might have to listen all the time to how good Jack is. I'm terrible in the carrier and good at the vet, and Lexy is good in the carrier and horrible at the vet.) The first thing Mommy told the cat doctor was that they wanted to check for a chip. No chip! Then the doctor asked what they wanted to do, and Will immediately said he'd keep him!

The doctor thinks Jack is a little over two years old. He's a boy, and he's neutered. The doctor checked to see if his boy parts didn't come down, and she's pretty sure they're not there, so he's definitely neutered. Boy, did Jack get mad when she did that! He got Advantage because he had "flea dirt" on him, got dewormed (which Will has to finish at home), got shots, and had blood work. His leukemia and FIV tests came back negative, but he was a little anemic so they took more blood and tomorrow the results will be in. They are pretty sure it's because he had fleas and because he is underweight (he weighs 7 pounds, but he's real skinny) and wasn't eating well on the street.

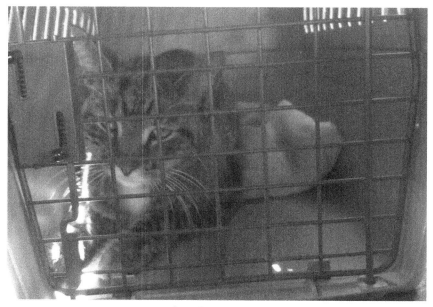

Jack on the way to the vet.

October 4, 2011

Lexy took over my spot on the bed last night and slept next to Mommy, and I was forced to sleep near the bottom of the bed. Insulting! That's my spot! OK, well, I admit I took over the bed after I moved in and became comfortable in my new home, but then it became MY spot. Now Lexy wants it back. I may need to hire a lawyer.

October 5, 2011

Guess where I slept last night? Right on top of Mommy! Then when she rolled over I stayed on one side of her and Lexy was on the other. We're going to have a problem when Will is here. He's going to have to sleep on the couch. Or he can have Lexy's box if he wants.

October 8, 2011

Do you know what Mommy did this morning? After she washed my food dish she almost opened a can of Lexy's food and put it in my dish. I don't eat that stuff! She quickly came to her senses and gave me my crunchy stuff. I can't imagine what got into her!

Mommy has been checking the Internet Lost and Found ads, but still nothing about a lost cat. She checked for the Bronx, Westchester, Manhattan, and Queens, just in case Jack travelled far, but so far nothing. One of my Facebook friends suggested that maybe Jack was a Bodega cat. Because of where Will works, this could very well be true. But Jack is safe now, and that's what counts.

Jack adopted a very good human and will have a very happy home. Welcome to the family Jack!

October 10, 2011

Jack went back to the vet today to get more blood work to check on his anemia. He got a clean bill of health! His red blood cell count numbers are up, so he's doing well! He gained 1.6 pounds and weighs 8.6 pounds. Way to go, Jack! He looks SO much better now; his anemia was probably because he didn't have nutritious food and because of those

pesky fleas. He is so happy now that he's saved. Look at this funny face he made at Mommy.

Jack making a funny face at Mommy.

Still Becoming Friends

October 14, 2011

Guess what? I tried to lick Lexy's nose and she wouldn't let me. Some nerve. So I went and licked Mommy's instead.

October 18, 2011

My friends just love seeing pictures of us. Today I posted this picture of Lexy and me looking out of the window. Well, I'm trying to anyway. Sometimes she's a window hog.

Lexy is hogging the window.

October 20, 2011

We got a box full of presents from Cindi Lou, Pinky, Willis, and Vinny today. We got three bags of Temptations treats, a bouncy mouse on a string and a bird that chirps! When Mommy threw the bird we thought a REAL bird was in the house and got big fat tails! MOL And Mommy got a Christmas ornament that says "Meowy Christmas." I'm lucky to have so many people and kitties care about me. Everyone loves Lexy, too. It's the best!

October 21, 2011

I have to go back to the cat doctor tomorrow, and I'm not happy about it. I was supposed to go next Thursday, but Mommy doesn't want to wait that long. I am very stuffy and am starting to sneeze a little more and a little harder. Yesterday morning she tried to give me a steam when she took a shower, but I wasn't having it. I carried on something terrible in the bathroom and even had a big fat tail. She finally got out of the shower and let me out. I don't like to be locked up anywhere at any time!

October 22, 2011

Mommy took this picture of me in the doctor's office because she thought I looked cute.

Mommy thought I looked cute in the doctor's office.

I don't know what's so cute about being in the doctor's office waiting to get a thermometer put "you know where." She probably wouldn't think it was so cute if it was her!

So now I have to have antibiotics AGAIN,

plus eye and nose drops. I lost about a half a pound, but the doctor says I'm far from underweight. This time I have to be on the medicines a little longer than usual to try to kick this out of my system. Who would have thought that stupid cold I got at the shelter would follow me all my life?

October 23, 2011

Mommy volunteered at an adoption event today, and five cats got homes! But they were all little cats; no adult cats got homes. Sigh...we need to spread the word about adopting adult cats. Adult cats make good companions, too! Even I'm doing what I can! I've been spending a lot of time posting about cats that need help, need a home, or are lost. Saving kitties is a tough job, but some cat has to do it.

October 29, 2012

Today is National Cat Day! I told my friends to remember to give their cat some extra hugs and kisses but also not to forget about the cats in need. I was one of them, and so was Lexy, and now we're living like princesses. OK, Lexy is the Queen, but I am a Princess.

October 30, 2011

Here are Lexy and me looking out of the window again this morning. This time she's sharing with me. OK, I won't lie. She usually shares with me, and Mommy sees us doing this almost every day. We both just

Sisters checking out the world together.

love the window. We have a lot of trees outside of our building and we love to watch the leaves blow in the wind. We also have squirrels that jump on the roof next door, and birds! Lots of birds that fly from tree to tree and rooftop to rooftop. We can sit for hours just watching the world.

November 2, 2011

Yes, Mommy, it is necessary to get a bath before you get out of bed in the morning. Do you want to go to work all dirty and smelly? You taught me a girl should always look her best, so don't complain.

November 3, 2011

Mommy is a little under the weather and is going to bed early, so I've been missing out on computer time. Hey! I have an idea! I can hold her mouth open and pop one of my pills in there to make her feel better. I wonder if I can get some of my friends to help me.

Who's that cute cat?

November 7, 2011

Who's that cat? She's kinda cute. Ohhh...that's me! Look how pretty my Sweet Pickles Designs collar is. How could it not be pretty with a name like The Lola?

November 8, 2011

Lexy taught me how to take my collar off. Mommy was waiting to leave the house and wasn't too happy that I wouldn't come out from under the bed so she could put it back on. People...they don't know how to have fun. Mommy needs to lighten up.

November 10, 2011

"I bet I could fit in there if I really tried. I bet I could."

I could fit in there.

I don't have the heart to tell her she can't. Plus, I want to laugh my whiskers off watching her try.

November 12, 2011

This morning, Lexy and I were lying on the bed and Mommy came in and sat down. Of course, I went over and gave her a lick hello. Then she gently brought me over by Lexy, and Lexy started licking my head. "See, you can be great friends," Mommy said. And then something happened... I won't keep you in suspense, I'll just tell you: Lexy bit my ear. Epic fail, Mommy, epic fail.

November 15, 2011

I had to write a letter to Mommy today. She doesn't listen to me when I meow at her, so I decided to put it in writing.

Dear Mommy,

At night when I'm sleeping on you or right next to you, could you lie still and not turn over so much? It makes me feel like I'm on the Cyclone at Coney Island. Plus, it makes it hard for me to keep you warm. That's my job.

Thanks.

Love, Lola

Facebook friends are asking how I know what the Cyclone ride feels like. Ummm... I guessed...it's not like I snuck out and went to Coney Island, or anything.

November 16, 2011

Uh, oh. I'm busted again. Mommy got a package in the mail today, and Lexy and I came to inspect it. As always, Mommy had to take the camera out, and she filmed us. Well, Lexy decided to lick my head, and I was nice to her and didn't swat her away. Now it's on film for the entire world to see. I have no secrets any more.

November 19, 2011

I told all of my Facebook friends that a local organization is offering free spaying/neutering services this week. I hope everybody realizes how important it is to do this for their pets. It's good for their health, and it cuts down on the stray and feral population. My hope is that everyone will realize how important it is to reduce that population so there are fewer animals suffering on the streets.

November 20, 2011

Lexy went to the cat doctor today, and she's not a happy camper. She got her rabies shot, and the vet told Mommy she has to brush her teeth because she has some tartar. She weighs a little over 11 pounds, and the doctor says she should lose a little bit of weight. That's because she STILL eats my food!

November 21, 2011

Mommy said taking her jewelry off of the dresser is one thing, but trying to steal it off her neck is another. I say she needs to share.

November 22, 2011

Mommy ignored me this morning when I was trying to wake her up. Then I sneezed. In her face. THAT got her attention!

November 23, 2011

Aunt Tamar gave Lexy a box, and it's her new favorite thing in the whole world. She naps in there for hours! I don't understand why she likes boxes so much, but I have to admit she looks pretty cute in it.

Lexy in her new favorite box.

Settled In At Last

November 27, 2011

This is our first Christmas together as a family, and my first real Christmas. Last year I was in the shelter, so that doesn't count at all. No cat can have a real Christmas in the shelter. This is Lexy's first real Christmas, too. Well, sort of. Last year she was here with Mommy, but they didn't put up a tree. The year before that she was in the shelter, and the year before that Mommy doesn't know where she was, but Lexy was a baby, she thinks.

Mommy took out all these pieces of stuff from a box and said it was a tree. It didn't look like a tree to me, but Lexy wanted to help Mommy put it together.

She likes to help with everything. That's because she's the inspector and nothing can go on in this house without her knowing about it and approving it. Then Mommy brought out all this cool stuff! Balls and other stuff that look like toys! She told us they are not toys; they are ornaments and NOT for playing. Yeah, right.

Waiting to help with the Christmas tree.

Lexy checked out the tree and gave it the all clear.

Having a tree is kinda cool, but having a family and a forever home is even better. Merry Christmas!

Lexy checked out the tree and it's fine.

November 29, 2011

Let me tell you, my sister is something else. Mommy walked into the kitchen today and saw her staring in the cabinet that she opened.

She is up to something for sure.

Lexy is up to something!

She took the treats! You're busted, Lexy!

December 2, 2011

We sent a bed to one of my Facebook friends, Harriet, and she got it today! Poor kitty is very scared in her new forever home. She has leukemia and has lived in a cage for a really long time. Now she's out of the cage but she's scared, so we sent her a bed that she can hide in. (Mommy says she hopes she uses it more than Lexy uses hers.) Her sister, Cindi Lou, got to keep the cool box. I love sending presents.

December 3, 2011

Mommy was thinking about what to get us for Christmas. She said we are very lucky cats because we have everything we could ask for. And we have lots of toys and treats we got from so many of our Facebook friends. So instead of buying us lots of presents, Mommy is going to make a donation to the shelter Lexy came from. Plus, she'll bring some stuff to a local shelter. I think that's a great present from us! We have to help the shelter animals.

December 4, 2011

I had to write a letter to Mommy today. She's got a lot of nerve sometimes.

Dear Mommy,
    Just because you can't find your earring doesn't mean you should look at me and say, "Lola, where is my earring?" The last time you saw it, it was in YOUR ear, not mine. I'm innocent. Maybe you shouldn't go to sleep with your jewelry on. Just an idea.
        Love,
        Lola

December 6, 2011

People love the letters I write to Mommy, and I got a couple of requests today. Here they are:

This one is for a couple of human friends who need one for their boss person:

Dear Boss Person,
    There's a lot of work stuff to do around here. A human can't possibly do all this stuff. I think if you put some of this work stuff away and give all the humans more of the green papers, it would be better. My idea will work. Trust me.
        Yours Truly,
        (Insert your name here).

They loved it! My barker friend Maizee Pearl asked me for this one:

Dear Mama,
    The tree skirt got all lumpy and bumpy and looked real messy. I'm sorry you got upset about it. I cannot tell a lie, Sarah did it. It wasn't this cute little face; only a cat could do that. And she had fun, too.
        Love,
        Maizee Pearl

Another success! And my kitty friend Pickles asked me for this one:

Dear Ma,

I'm sorry I got you so worried when I went on my adventure around the neighborhood. I'm such a curious kitty, and I love excitement. I just wanted to do some research on new collar ideas for the business. I know I'm grounded and can't go outside at all till I can recite my phone number, but you should know I can't do that because I'm a cat and humans won't understand what I'm meowing. I have a better idea: take my box away for a week and I'll do extra hours at the office, too. Then we can go out with my harness and I can roll around in the grass.

    Thanks.
      Love,
      Pickles

I'm getting pretty good at this!

December 9, 2011

I'm in trouble. I took off my collar and Mommy can't find it. She says now I don't have any ID. Now, that's the whole point of hiding my collar! No ID means I never have to leave the house again!

December 12, 2011

Yesterday Lexy left me alone the whole day and didn't bother me at all. It was wonderful. Now today she's started chasing me around the house again! Can't I get a break? When will she realize I'm not a cat's cat, I'm a people cat? Mommy still hopes that she'll see us cuddling together some day. I don't know about that.

December 13, 2011

I wrote another letter to Mommy today:

Dear Mommy,

If you're going to give me my medicines, I think you should get it right. I get the liquid stuff once a day, the pill twice a day, and the paste twice a day. I DO NOT get the liquid stuff twice a day. Maybe you should read the labels better. Then I probably won't spit so much of that orange yucky stuff all over your work pants. Or maybe you could just not give them to me at all. Just a suggestion.

> *Thanks.*
> *Love,*
> *Lola*

December 14, 2011

Well, my suggestion to Mommy didn't work. She decided to get it right and give me my medicines the right way.

December 15, 2011

Mommy says George Clooney is the bomb-diggity. I don't know what that is, but it must be good since he adopted a shelter dog! Yes! Another shelter animal saved! Thank you, George Clooney, whoever you are.

December 16, 2011

Mommy is so sad about the pets that have gone to the Rainbow Bridge recently and those that are sick. She's also sad about all the animals that need rescue and how there aren't enough people who help. She gave Lexy and me big hugs when she got home. She hugged me so hard I squeaked!

December 17, 2012

We got a package in the mail today from Aunt Colleen! (That's Shelby, Aggie, and Calculus Q. Jones's mom.) Oh, it was filled with so many goodies for me, Lexy, and Mommy, too! Lexy and I got Party Mix treats (which were just yummy), and Christmas toys that make crinkly noises when we play with them. One is a penguin, and the other is a gingerbread man. Mommy also got presents with candy she said is delish.

P.S. Mommy said we are getting more Christmas cards than she is!

December 19, 2011

Today is a sad day. One year ago today Will's cat, Tiger, went to the Rainbow Bridge. Smooches and hugs, Tiger. I know you're watching down on us. And you sent Jack to Will so he wouldn't be lonely.

December 20, 2011

Mommy is done with school for the semester! But she told me I can't be on Facebook much tonight because she has "stuff to do." Pffffttt...Stuff...my social life is more important than stuff.

December 25, 2011

Merry Christmas! Last year I was a lonely kitty in a shelter and this year I have the best home and the best friends!

My first Christmas in my forever home.

December 26, 2011

Lexy thinks she's British. She's celebrating Boxing Day by hanging out in this big box Mommy got a present in. She thinks every day should be Boxing Day, because she loves boxes so much. (Lexy never met a box she didn't like.)

Lexy celebrating Boxing Day.

December 30, 2011

I told my friends today that I'm going to write a book. I was nervous to tell people, because I wasn't sure people would want to read my life story, my autobiography, my memoire. But guess what? I got a lot of support, and they said they couldn't wait to read it!

Mommy cleaned today—I mean, she REALLY cleaned, and I didn't like it one bit. I'm not used to that! Watching her work so hard really wore me out, so when she was finally done I had to take a little nap.

Watch cat on patrol.

December 31, 2011

One year ago, today I was a sick kitty lying in a cage in the shelter. Today I can sleep in the sun on my favorite chair. Life is good. Don't forget to be grateful for the blessings in your life!

Life is good.

85

January 2, 2012

Today I posted on Facebook that my New Year's wish is for all animals to be treated with love and respect, and for all the street cats to get saved and have warm homes filled with yummy treats, sunbeams to sleep in, and lots of cuddles and head scratches. So many humans responded and said they feel the same way! I'm so glad they understand, and I hope that they keep telling their friends and families and spread the word so more people get involved.

Squishing Lexy's bag.

January 3, 2011

Today I sat on Lexy's bag and squished it. It's a good thing she didn't see me.

January 5, 2012

One year ago today I was discovered in the shelter. Aunt Leslie saw me lying so sick in my cage and started her campaign to save me. It was the start of my rescue.

January 6, 2012

Today is a very, very special day, and I'll tell you why. (Listen closely) Ahem... One year ago today I WAS RESCUED FROM THE SHELTER! The shelter released me to Aunt Leslie, and she took me to the hospital where they started me on my road to recovery. I never again had to worry about "Death Row." Smooches and hugs to you, Aunt Leslie!

I can't believe it has been a whole year since my rescue. I am so thankful for the life I have now, and I love my home so much. I am the happiest and luckiest cat in the whole world! I wish all shelter cats could celebrate their own rescue day. Maybe it could be a National Holiday!

January 7, 2012

Mommy saw Aunt Leslie today! I don't like to go out, or I would have joined them. But she gave me a BIG hug from her when she got home. I heard Mommy showed Aunt Leslie some notes we've been making about my book and she loved it! This is so exciting!

January 8, 2012

Mommy is paying bills today. Yawn...that's so boring! I'm sure she'd have much more fun playing with me.

January 10, 2012

Today I wrote another letter for Pickles to her doggie brother, Rocky.

Yawn!

Dear Rocky,

Dood, you are such a huge man dog. You're all buff and stuff with a shiny coat, and you have all the girl dogs turning their heads to look at you. I know you want to keep that awesome bod you have, so I decided I'd help you out. From time to time I'm going to eat a very tiny bit of food from your bowl so you don't have so many calories to eat. I'm a little tiny cat compared to you, so my tiny bit is only a small morsel for you. But you're still saving calories and I'm helping you stay in shape. Look at those biceps! Dood, you're a body builder.

See what a good cat sister I am?

> *Love,*
> *Pickles*

I'm the best letter writer I know!

January 12, 2012

The cat is out of the bag. The past few nights, Lexy has been jumping on me when I'm sleeping on the bed. She's waking me up to play! I used to ignore her and run up by Mommy's head, but lately I've decided to be generous to her so I jump off and let her chase me. Last night Lexy woke Mommy up by running around the bedroom and jumping on the furniture, and like always when Mommy turned over she felt around to see where I was so she didn't squish me. But when she was petting me I heard Lexy make a noise, and I sat up on full alert. And then, well, I just had to run off the bed to go find her, and we started running around. When I came back to bed Mommy said, "Miss Lola, you are BUSTED! You like playing with Lexy, you big faker." After almost a whole year I'm starting to play with her! But now what am I going to do when I want to pretend she's bothering me? Mommy is on to me; she's getting too smart.

January 13, 2012

Oh boy, Mommy is in T-R-O-U-B-L-E! Lexy is mad and she posted this on my Facebook page today:

> *This is Lexy, and I feel I must post today. I am very upset with Mother. This morning she was running late, and I had to wait for my breakfast. She actually had the nerve to take a shower, get dressed, and do her makeup before she fed me. She had her coffee, but I had to deal with a rumbling belly. And when I went into the bathroom to complain loudly, all she had to say was, "Lexy, I'll feed you before I leave. If you girls didn't wake me up at 3:40 a.m., I wouldn't be running late." Her inability to go back to sleep is not my problem. Even worse, when I rolled around on the floor to show her my belly and say good morning, she ignored me! I'm afraid I have no choice but to report her. Now what did I do with Aunt Leslie's phone number? She won't like it one bit to hear her BFF was ignored and my needs weren't met. Lola, get me that cell phone!*

Uh oh, I better hide under the bed, because I'm not getting involved in this.

A Happy Ending

January 16, 2011

Today is a day that should go down in history. (It should go down in CATSTO-RY!). Today is my Adoptiversary! One year ago today Mommy and Will picked me up from the hospital and took me home! Mommy gave me a hug this morning and told me she's so proud of the young girl cat I have grown into and that I'm becoming so brave about life. Then I went and hid under the coffee table.

I'm so grateful for my friends who have been here through my journey from being confined in my suite when I was sick, to learning to get along with Lexy, through all of my cat doctor visits and sneezes, and all my funny posts. I love them all and look forward to another fun-filled year!

Rescue Stories

Lexy

Mommy doesn't know a whole lot about Lexy, but I can tell you what I've heard. My human cousin Aaliyah got a puppy for Christmas in 2009 (that's my doggie cousin, Diesel). In April 2010, Mommy was in Petco with some of our family to buy puppy stuff for him, and while she was walking around the store looking for presents for Diesel she saw the adoption table. Mommy had always loved kitties, so she went to look at them.

She was checking out all the kitties when she saw a beautiful black-and-white cat sitting calmly in her cage. This cat reminded her of one she had many years ago, Marvin, that was her baby. She called Auntie Ruthie over to look and said, "Who does this remind you of?" and of course Auntie Ruthie said she looked just like Marvin. The volunteer told Mommy her name was Lexy, and she was a great and friendly cat. Mommy was told Lexy had been there a year. "Why?" Mommy wanted to know. She was wondering if there was something wrong with her. The volunteer told her Lexy is very friendly and sweet, but she often got passed by for a kitten or a more exotic looking cat. (That makes me mad!)

Mommy opened the cage to pet her, and Lexy was so nice! Mommy was told that Lexy loves to play. He said whenever he walks passed her cage she sticks her paw out to touch him and play. (Lexy still does that—she sits on the kitchen chair and sticks her paw out to play with Mommy.) The volunteer said she's affectionate and would definitely be a lap cat. A lap cat! Mommy hadn't had a cat in a while and would love a lap cat! Mommy felt bad because all she could picture in her mind was Lexy sitting in a cage on display every weekend for a whole year. How sad. She had to get her out!

There was also another woman there who was interested in Lexy and was going to let them know if she could take her. Well, Mommy wasn't having that. She had already fallen in love with Lexy and wanted to take her home.

Mommy talked about it to Auntie Ruthie and our cousins on the way home, and there was only one problem: her landlord. She had been told she was not allowed pets when she moved in six years earlier. All the way home to Queens, Mommy thought about Lexy and even told Will about her. She dug her lease out of the closet to see what it said, and there it was, stamped in big black letters: "NO PETS." Oh no...Mommy just had to have Lexy. What was she going to do?

She knew a couple of people in the building had cats, but they had lived there before our landlord bought the building, so their cats were "grandfathered" in. Hmmm, what to do, what to do? Mommy decided to call the landlord and ask him if she could have a pet. She figured, what's the worst that could happen? All he could say was no. When Mommy called him, he told her she's a good tenant and he wants her to be happy, so yes, she could have a cat! Mommy was so happy she could have Lexy!

She immediately emailed the shelter and found out that Lexy was still available! She filled out the application and waited. And waited. The person in charge couldn't reach Mommy's references, so they wanted to contact the vet Mommy used 15 years ago in Rockland County—15 years ago! Mommy was getting nervous that they wouldn't give Lexy to her. After emails back and forth, Mommy sent this one: "I am very much a pet lover and Lexy will have a wonderful loving home. I've already gone to the pet store to buy everything she would need. She will definitely be well cared for with me, I can assure you." And guess what the next email said? "OK, she's all yours then!" Yay! It seems since Lexy was such a favorite they wanted to make sure she went to a good home.

The very next day was Saturday, so Mommy went back to the pet store with Auntie Ruthie and my cousins (they all wanted to see Lexy). Lexy did very well on the ride home. She ended up being in the car for almost two hours! At first she was meowing, but Mommy put some nice jazz music on and she calmed down (Mommy always puts that music on now when Lexy is in the car).

As soon as they got home, Mommy showed Lexy her food and litter box. Lexy had to pee; good thing she made it to Queens! Here's a picture of Lexy when she got home.

Lexy's first day at home.

92

She just knew she was going to be the Queen!

Her first night there, Lexy sat on Mommy's bed all night. She didn't lie down; she just sat with her head up. Whenever she got down, Mommy went to check on her, so Mommy didn't sleep much. But she didn't care; she was happy to give Lexy a good home.

On Lexy's second day at home, something happened that made her SO scared. Mommy had already planned to go out and buy a new TV that day, so she kept her plans. When she and Will came home with the TV, there was some commotion in the house. Some furniture had to be moved and stuff like that. Lexy got so scared she ran and hid under the bed for HOURS! Mommy could only get her out by bringing her some tuna fish. Poor Lexy! For a few months Lexy would hide whenever Mommy moved stuff around, even just the laundry or stuff like that. I can't even imagine my brave sister hiding, so she must have been really, really scared. Mommy said after about four months that stopped and Lexy took her throne as Queen.

You know what else Lexy used to do when she moved in? She REALLY used to bother Mommy at night. Lexy would start to wake Mommy up at around 3 a.m! She'd run around the room and scratch the furniture, or she'd jump on the bed and run around the bed. And she would scratch the box spring, too. The funny part is that if Mommy got up and lay down on the couch, Lexy would stop. As long as Mommy wasn't in bed she was OK. Eventually Lexy made the time later and later... 4:00, 5:00, 6:00, and then stopped. She doesn't do that anymore.

Lexy is a funny cat and did some funny stuff. The best is that she would take her treats from the cupboard and open the package. One day Mommy was at the computer, and Lexy came out of the bathroom licking her lips. Mommy said "What are you eating?!" She was afraid to go look in the bathroom, because she was afraid she would find a mouse or something. But what she found was Lexy's package of treats. Lexy snuck it right past her! Then another time Mommy heard a noise in the kitchen and found this:

Lexy learned how to open the cabinet to get the treats.

93

And another time, this!

Found the treats again!

Mommy put her treats in a container, but that didn't work, either.

Now they're up high where she can't get them. Mommy says someday soon Lexy will be able to open a can of food!

Mommy tried piecing together Lexy's past, based on her conversations with the volunteer at the shelter about her "abandonment," and Lexy's behaviors when she got

Nothing can come between Lexy and her food.

94

her home. Mommy thinks Lexy's family moved and left her behind. My poor sister! At one vet appointment, Lexy was so terrified she was trembling, and the vet asked Mommy if she knew anything about her past. The vet felt bad and was concerned, but Mommy didn't really have any information to give her. After that appointment, Lexy was not herself for two days. The first night she sat on the floor all night and would not go sleep on anything high up or comfy. The next day she wouldn't let Mommy near her. Usually Lexy has a deep meow, but when Mommy tried to pick her up she meowed this little "mew mew mew" meow that was so sad. She didn't even want to eat, and she threw up. The day after that, she started to come around and met Mommy at the door and let her pet her. After that she was her old self again. How sad is that? My poor sister!

So the magic question is this: Is Lexy a lap cat like Mommy was told? Nope! Lexy has never, not once, sat on Mommy's lap. She doesn't like to be held, and Mommy has to sneak hugs. But Mommy doesn't care that Lexy doesn't sit on her lap because she's funny and sweet and Mommy knows she loves her.

So there you have it, that's Lexy's story. I think we both got lucky and adopted a great mother who loves us to pieces.

Lola White
Queens, NY

Sheba and Max

Beautiful Sheba

My Husband, Steve, and I rescued our first senior-kittizen in 2006. Her name was Sheba and she found herself at Cats Protection after her elderly owner had died and none of the family could take her in. She was 15 years old. My husband vowed he was having nothing to do with a cat and declared he wasn't going to be cleaning her litter tray or feeding her. That was my job. (He didn't especially like cats.)

Sheba arrived at her new home on a Sunday afternoon in June. Steve was the one who sat on the floor with her in the utility room that we had designated has her safe spot, and talked to her for the first couple of hours after her arrival. It was the start of a three-year love affair I couldn't possibly compete with! Sheba greeted us every day when we came home from work by bounding down the stairs, begging to be picked up by her Daddy. He always obliged and usually spent the first half-hour home cradling Sheba in his arms and talking about how he should make her a sling so he could carry her around for longer.

She slept in her basket at the top of the stairs and would call down to us in the living room when she wanted play time. We would oblige her by pausing the television and going upstairs to play through the bars of the stair rail or with her bouncy balls until

96

she tired. She was pretty sprightly for an elderly lady, and her medication for arthritis was all she really needed to keep her going.

When Steve went upstairs to prepare for bed at night, Sheba would sit up in her basket and wait eagerly for him to enter the bedroom and then jump on the bed, stomping around impatiently until he was horizontal and she could assume her favourite position: in the middle of his chest, with her paw on his chin.

In September 2009, Sheba stopped eating and not even her favourite prawns could tempt her. We took her to the vet immediately, and she was diagnosed with liver disease. Her illness coincided with Steve's new job, which took him away from London to Dusseldorf during the week. Sheba was hospitalized for 10 days on a drip in an effort to improve her condition, but there was nothing that could be done. She came home to us on a Friday afternoon to wait for her Daddy to come back home so that he could say goodbye. That weekend we had the vet come to our home to put our precious girl to sleep. We laid her to rest at the bottom of the garden. We were devastated, broken, and vowed never to have another cat—it was just too painful to say goodbye.

I donated everything that was Sheba's, save her basket and food bowls, to Cats Protection because I couldn't bear to see any reminders of her around the house. It hurt too much. The basket and food bowls were relegated to the loft. The house was a sad and empty place.

On October 12, 2009, a neighbour contacted me to say she had found a sickly old cat down the road from us and that the cat was at the local vet, where he'd been for a couple of weeks. She asked if I might consider taking him in or if I could help her find a home for him because, as a flight attendant, she was not home enough to take on the responsibility. Attempts to find his owners had proved futile, none of the rescues would take him in because of his poor health, and the vet had given him until the weekend before they were going to put him to sleep. What could I do? I volunteered to foster him, but I was adamant I was just a stepping stone for him. I was NOT going to love him.

He was in a shocking state, even after 2 weeks at the vet: weeping eyes, ulcers in his mouth bleeding and oozing pus, and feces matting his fur from constant diarrhea. He was totally neglected when found, un-neutered and un-chipped. There was no way he could have been someone's beloved pet. The vet told us he thought he was about 12-15 years old and that he had oral cancer and was unlikely to live beyond a few months. His raggedy ear led us to assume he'd been something of a gladiator in his youth, and we wanted to give him a fighting chance, so we named the old boy Maximus Decipuss Meridius after Russell Crowe's character in the Gladiator movie, and brought him home to foster him.

On his first weekend with us, in an effort to spruce him up a bit, we tried to wash him with a leave-in foaming shampoo for cats. We lathered him up and rubbed him up and down until he was soaked to the skin. I'm not sure it helped with the smell, but he purred himself silly loving the attention.

Not sure what to do with a litter tray, Max would often do his business alongside it, so during the day when I was at work, and at night, his home was the utility room, where the tiled floor was carpeted with newspaper and he had a hooded basket to sleep in. My first jobs in the morning and when I got home from work were to clean up any "Maxi-dents" and to try and coax Max to eat. I would make him rice and fish or rice and chicken—foods recommended to treat his diarrhea—and I would sit on the floor next to him, stroking him in order to encourage him to eat. In the evenings, we would sit on the sofa, Max purring on a blanket on my lap. Despite his obvious discomfort, he wanted to be cuddled and loved. And despite my resolve, I couldn't help but fall in love with him. As Max began to fill the Sheba-shaped void in my heart, I stopped fooling myself that I was just fostering him.

It took time, patience, and the right vet to get Maxi's condition under control, and a grooming session under anesthetic to get him properly clean. He was the most stoic cat I have ever encountered. Motivated by treats, Max would willingly open his mouth so we could give him his liquid medication, which we syringed into his mouth twice a day. He put up with having his eyes cleaned, his mouth wiped during meals, and his nose cleaned during occasional bouts of colds. He wasn't so keen on having his paws cleaned, but even then, all he would do was gently push your hand away. He had the sweetest, most gentle nature and he loved to be cuddled. I would hold him in my arms, where he would purr himself to sleep and lie there for as long as I would let him.

Maxi loved his garden and would lie out there in all kinds of weather, so we rigged up plastic sheeting over a sun umbrella so he didn't get soaked in the summer rain. We drew the line at letting him spend too much time outdoors in the winter, but he would beg to go out the moment he saw a patch of sunlight. He liked to watch the birds and let them steal his food, which he trained me to serve him al fresco.

It wasn't until we'd had Max for 15 months and he ran away from home while we were on holiday that we discovered he had not been a stray at all, but someone's pet. Someone that didn't think cats needed medical attention, and who thought when he went missing, that he'd just gone off to die, or had been eaten by a fox, so they didn't bother trying to find him. That "someone" lived less than a kilometer from our home and only meters away from where Max had been found. They responded to our lost posters to tell us that Max was their "Batty." We learned that he was 16 years old and that they had got him and his brother for their young boys, who had named them Batman and

Robin. Robin had been killed by a car some years earlier. We thought we might have a custody battle, but when they discovered the medication regimen and care that Max required, his previous family decided he would be best off remaining in our care. We heaved a sigh of relief, resisted the urge to mete out some justice on them, and carried on with the business of loving our boy.

We lost our beloved Maxi in early 2012 to cancer, but in the short time we were privileged enough to have him in our lives he became something of a celebrity, with over 1,400 friends following his antics on Facebook. Not only did everyone who met him in person fall in love with him, but so also did everyone who got to experience his big personality through the Internet. Testament to this is the fact that his memorial fund raised over £1000 for Cats Protection so that other cats will have a chance to be rescued and share their love with someone in their forever home. Rescue a cat, there is no greater reward!

Lynn Pacella
Surrey, UK

Beloved Max

You can read more about Max on his Facebook page: https://www.facebook.com/Maxipuss. (Max was one of Lola's and Lexy's best friends.)

Pickles

If you had known me three years ago, you would know one thing: I was a dog person. Yes, that's right; I was not a cat person at all, but crazy about dogs. I mean, don't get me wrong, I was and am a total animal person, sometimes a little over the top. I'm the one who rents out dog daycares for our dogs' birthdays parties and invites everyone I know. I volunteered at a vet for years and am still a volunteer at the Oregon Humane Society. I've even had a pet hamster. But because I had never had a cat of my own, I never thought I would. That and the fact that my boyfriend Morgan and I have three large (all over 65lb) dogs. I never thought a cat would want to live with all of us. But that all changed one warm September day in 2009.

Morgan and I were heading down to Eugene, Oregon, to help my little brother move. We were about halfway from Portland to Eugene when we drove by an exit ramp where a litter of kittens and their mom had been stranded on the grass between the freeway and the off ramp. I couldn't believe my eyes: there, on the side of Interstate 5, were four kittens and their mom. I didn't know what we were supposed to do, but I knew we had to turn around and try to rescue them. After an hour of chasing four kittens on the side of the freeway, we could only catch the mom and the one black-and-white kitten. We didn't know what to do; honestly the other three kittens were super fierce and wanted nothing to do with us. It was getting dangerous and we knew something bad could easily happen if they ran out to the road.

I don't know how long we went back and forth about what to do, but it seemed like hours. After all the chasing, the one thing we knew for sure was that we couldn't catch the other kittens ourselves. They were just too fast and a little too feral. We didn't think we should take the mom because they were still nursing, and we didn't know what to do with the black-and-white one who seemed like she really wanted to get the heck out of there. It was one of the hardest decisions I have ever had to make: do we split up this family since it is an awful situation and rescue the one we can, or do we leave them all? In the end, after she jumped back in the car, we decided that she was coming home with us.

We left, thinking that we would be able to find a rescue or someone who knew what they were doing to go back for the rest. However, after calling all the rescues, shelters, and even the sheriff in the area, no one would go out and get them. It was heartbreaking. I don't know what ever happened to the rest of the litter and it still brings tears to my eyes just thinking about, but I do hope someone else was able to rescue them.

I don't know if it was the determined look in her eyes or the total trust she seemed to have in us, but I could tell this little black-and-white kitten was a special little kitty. We brought her home thinking that we would take her to the vet, get her healthy, and find her a home. Seriously, what little kitten would want to live with three large dogs? We have a finished basement and we made her a fortress of her own, equipped with a baby gate to keep the dogs out. When I came home from work the next day, the kitten had jumped the baby gate and was on the couch cuddling with the

Pickles after being rescued.

dogs. Within seconds, I knew she was staying and still to this day all four of them have the most amazing bond. I've never seen anything like it—they all love each other so much.

It took a few days to pick a name for her, but we eventually deicide Pickles was the perfect name, seeing as how she had already been in so many pickles in her short life. After she had a name, I went out looking for a tag and collar for her. I have always been obsessed with collars (our dogs had endless supplies), and it was kind of my thing you know, dressing the dogs in fancy collars. I was super-excited to go pick out my first cat collar. I had no idea what to expect, but figured it was the same as the dog collar selections. Boy, was I wrong. I couldn't believe the awful selections the pet stores and boutiques had for cats. They were so bad, I didn't even want to buy any of the ones I found after going to almost every pet shop in Portland. I did end up buying one with dragonflies printed on it so she could have identification, but I was not happy with it at all and decided I was going to try to make her a collar that I liked.

Pickles and her best friend forever, Lola

Well, the first major problem was I had no idea how to sew. I went to school for advertising and I'm a commercial real estate broker. Sewing was one of those things I never had interest in before, so I really had little to fall back on. Thank goodness for YouTube and one of our dogs' love for pillows. My parents had given me a sewing machine a couple of months before for my birthday to help with the pillows that kept getting chewed, but it was still in the box and I didn't even know how to thread it. So I unpacked it, logged on to YouTube, and taught myself how to sew. It was a little sketchy at first, and I will never show anyone the first collars I made, but I figured it out and Pickles was finally wearing a collar that I loved. After several months of playing with designs and filling Pickles's closet, I decided it was time to see if other people liked them too. On April 20, 2010, Pickles and I opened our very own Etsy Shop, Sweet Pickles Designs.

So far it's been a wild ride, but it has been so incredibly fun and exciting. When watching YouTube over and over trying to learn what a bobbin was, I never thought all this was possible. We have met so many amazing people and cats through our short journey so far, and they inspire me every day to keep doing what we are doing. Currently, we have collars in over 20 pet boutiques worldwide, some as far away as Sweden, Australia, and Singapore.

So now, here we are almost three years later, and if you ask my friends they would now say I am the definition of a crazy cat lady and that my world revolves around cats. I never would have thought it was possible before, but I'm proud to be a flag-toting, cat-shirt wearing, crazy cat lady in love with a little black-and-white cat I found on the side on Interstate 5. Pickles is my everyday wingman, Sweet Pickles's CEO, and the face of the company. I wouldn't have it any other way, and I'm happier than I've ever been.

I absolutely love my job and hope Pickles and I will be designing fashion for all our cat friends around the world for many, many more years to come.

Meows!

Shana Freimark
Portland, OR

Follow Pickles's antics on her Facebook page: https://www.facebook.com/CEO.Pickles

And don't forget to follow Sweet Pickles Designs (https://www.facebook.com/Sweet-PicklesDesigns) for tips on having the best dressed cat.

Donovan

One morning in September 2002, I was on my way to work at 5:00 a.m. I stopped at a nearby fast food restaurant to get breakfast at the drive thru, and as I pulled in to place my order, I saw a small kitten with a dark face, paws, and tail, sitting patiently at the back door. Obviously this kitten knew where to get food. But it was so small and tiny. Where was its mama? How did it get there?

I backed my car up. (Luckily, at that time of morning, there wasn't anyone else pulling up to the drive thru.) As I got out to see about this tiny baby, it took off. Once again, I was glad there weren't any other cars coming. After the kitten disappeared into the morning darkness, I placed my order and went on to work.

As I started my job, something kept nagging at me about that kitten. How old was it? Where was its mother? Was it all alone? Had someone "thrown it out"? My job started at 6:00 a.m. and my shift wasn't over until 4:30 p.m., and that kitten stayed in my heart all day.

As I drove home that afternoon, I decided to go back to that fast food place and see if anyone knew anything. I talked to the manager, and he said that there were "at least six or eight kittens" and that they fed them on a regular basis. And they all had dark faces, paws, and tails. I walked around the parking lot for a bit and saw a big trash pile next to dumpster a few feet away. And sure enough, one of the kittens appeared. It was on that day that my journey into animal rescue began, and little did I know that one of those kittens would be the love of my life.

I went home and got out the phone book looking for animal rescues and found The Ark of Cleveland (TN). I called and told the man who answered (who turned out to be the director) what I had found and asked if he could help me rescue them. We met there the next afternoon and as we talked, one of the kittens again made an appearance. Then another, and another. Some were bigger than others, indicating there may be more than one litter of brothers and sisters. But no sign of a mother cat. Luckily, he agreed to help. We set out humane traps and over the next few weeks trapped eight kittens and, finally, their mother. She was a Russian Blue and didn't look like any of her babies.

The very first kitten to be trapped was the one I had first seen that morning at the back door of the restaurant. I told the man that I wanted that one. There was just something about it.

They all went to the vet and got everything they needed. Amazingly, none had fleas or worms or anything associated with living outside, and they were healthy! The day came for me to pick up the one I wanted. The director called and said "The one you want is a boy and he needs a name." Oh my. I hadn't even thought about that. I sat for a minute... "Donovan " I said. "His name is Donovan."

As I drove to the director's home, many thoughts went through my head. Could I afford another cat? I already had one at home. What would she think about a new cat? We had been together for three years, just she and I. And being single and living on one income, having another cat was something I'd never even considered. But then the image of that little baby sitting at the back door waiting for food went through my head again. Actually, he hadn't been out of my head this whole time.

I pulled into the driveway, got out the carrier, and went to the door. The director let me in and took me to where Donovan was being kept. And there he was, the most beautiful thing I'd ever seen. Only four months old, rolling over and over, and flopping down in front of my feet. I scooped him up, placed him in the carrier, and took him home. And I've been in love with him ever since.

He has grown into a big beautiful ragdoll, weighing in now at 18 pounds.

I've often been told how lucky he was that I found him. But, truth be told, he found me and I'm the lucky one. I found the love of my life and his name is Donovan.

Sherry Black
Etowah, TN

Handsome Donovan

Mitzi

For several years I would kitty-sit a neighbor's cat when they went out of town. One night in January 2006, I let myself into the house and went into the living room. The light by the front window was on, and there was a kitten looking in the window! She was a tortie and had a striking strip of rust-colored fur on her forehead. Throughout the evening I played with her by tapping my finger on the glass while she batted at it with her paw from the other side. I was in love! The next day I saw her on the front porch and tried to catch her a couple times, but she ran away through the snow. When the family returned, I asked about the kitten, and they said she had been there for quite a while and they had been feeding her.

In March of that year, the mom of the family called to tell me they had to catch the kitten because male cats were going after her. I told her that if the kitten was caught to bring her over to my house. At 8:15 p.m. on March 15, 2006, the doorbell rang and there was my neighbor holding a pet carrier. She had tricked the kitten into going into the carrier by putting food in it. I whisked it into the house; when I opened the carrier, a very scared little kitty ran out and under the futon. I got a plastic tub and put litter in it, and put some food and water in bowls. I realized that she had never used a litter box before but I thought, well, she's small, so there won't be much to clean up.

The next morning I went into the front bedroom and was quite pleased to see that the kitten had used the litter box. She was smart! After work that day, I found her under the futon, against the wall. I had to lie down on my stomach and stretch as far as I could to reach her and pull her out. It seemed like she had never been held by a human before, and I cuddled her for the next hour and a half straight! Two weeks later, the vet determined she was about 5-1/2 months old when she came into my house because her adult fangs were coming in.

At first I named the kitten Samantha, but it just didn't feel right. A couple days later I was washing dishes and thinking about all the cats I had in my life. I remembered a cat we had had when I was very young who was named Mitzi and I knew that should be her name.

Mitzi was a very smart cat, and playful throughout her life. One day she jumped up on the couch and dropped her kooshball-type toy next to me. For some reason I picked it up and threw it and she retrieved it! Mitzi and I played fetch every day after that.

In May of 2011, I noticed Mitzi making noise when she was breathing. I took her to the vet, and she was found to have a tumor in her throat. It was fast-growing and she would not have survived the waiting while a biopsy was done so she was helped to The Rainbow Bridge. Although she lived only 5-1/2 years, I am happy knowing that I was able to rescue her from life on the street and give her a happy home. She brought a lot of joy to my life in that short time.

Mitzi and her toy.

Lisa Krolasik
Milwaukee, WI

Princess Pockets

When I was working at a vet's office, a couple brought in a two-week-old kitten, who had obviously been abandoned by her mother. She was covered in ant bites, and her eyes and ears weren't open. On my lunch, I bought a nursing bottle and formula for her even though my boss at the time had forbidden me to take on the baby. When the office closed, I went back to get the baby I had hidden away. She was so tiny she fit in the pocket of my scrub top, hence the name Pockets.

We drove home that night doing 35 MPH because I didn't want anything to happen to her. I had gotten her home and set about bottle feeding. For the first couple of weeks, it was touch and go. Luckily she didn't develop any illness or contract anything, which sent me over the moon. After about a month, I was called to my boss's office for counseling and three days later I was fired for taking a cat in. Princess was worth it.

Princess Pockets turned nine years old May 3, 2014 and is a rambunctious, healthy, happy, ROYALLY spoiled baby girl. I think of her as my daughter; I bottle-fed her, kept her safe, and made sure she went to the bathroom so she wouldn't get sick. She received the title of Princess because she is so sweet and loving. If you're upset, she's right in your face on the bed, making sure you are OK. She loves to play fetch with paper balls and loves to cuddle. She is, in my eyes, one of the truest rescues there is: Left for death by her own mother and then brought to the vet's by a kind-hearted person—and the rest is history. To be nursed back to health and survive is a miracle within itself. She is now a happy tubby 12 pounds with bright eyes and a truly bushy tail! She's a medium hair calico, and her motor, oh my gracious, it puts drag racing cars to shame. She sits on my desk watching the world and clicking her little heart out when a bird comes close to the window. My ant-bitten, abandoned, scared baby has turned into a gorgeous animal. She is my true daughter, aside from the obvious fact I didn't birth her!

Princess Pockets is not only my child but also the love of my life. She makes me happy when I'm sad. The BEST thing in the world is coming home and getting a fluffy hug from my one and only baby girl. If I leave home for any extended period of time, she will camp out in my room while she waits for my return. Her spot in my room is either on the desk to watch the birds or on my pillows above my head. She makes me so immensely happy beyond words. We watch TV together (disagreements on channels do happen!) and it's just simply amazing. She is also an EXCELLENT spider hunter and killer, which is perfect (since I have a serious case of arachnophobia), so waking up some days to an expired spider melts my heart. She's getting chunky in her old age but that's OK, there's more to hug!

Princess Pockets is TRULY one of the best things to have ever happened to me; getting fired to save her was so worth it and I would do it again in a heartbeat, no questions asked. I love her, I cherish her, and I respect her. She truly is one of a kind, and she's all mine.

Princess Poickets relaxing.

Ansley & Princess Pockets Crook
Odessa FL

Lucky

Lucky wasn't lucky when I adopted him in April 2012. It was a hot day as usual in the outskirts of Semarang, Indonesia. My employees and I were purchasing a banner for our office. Just as we were going home, I saw the store employee bring out a tiny kitten to be thrown away to the busy streets. The kitten was barely a month old and was just alone. So I exclaimed to the employee, "What do you think you are doing? Give the kitten to me!" It was instinctual for me to bring home the kitten and nurse him back to health before deciding what to do. I immediately hugged him, yet he was screaming loudly and wanting to escape. Regardless, I went home with him.

Lucky after being rescued.

The first night was sleepless for me: I set up warm bottles under some blankets for him to lie on, I helped him pee by rubbing his belly, and even coaxed him to eat some chows I had prepared for the other cat I had in the house. He drank and ate nothing, and

I stayed at his side the whole night and worried. The very next day, however, he was exploring the whole house, played with my hand, and even stuck his head in the food that I was bringing for my other cat.

Lucky and friend.

What my two cats have taught me:

1. Anything can be made beautiful with love and determination.
2. Humans must protect animals because we have the power to.
3. Anything is possible.

I think writing this story is the most meaningful thing I have ever done in my life.

Andry Soenario
Indonesia

Tallulah Jane

I'm an artist who paints cats (www.lesliecobb.com). In September 2003, I was in my booth at an Art and Wine Festival when a young woman came in holding a miniscule kitten. She explained that the shelter where she volunteered had scheduled the kitten for euthanasia, and so she brought her home even though her rental unit did not allow pets. She had assumed she'd be able to find another home for the kitten, but after three days the landlord was threatening her with eviction if she didn't immediately get rid of the cat. She had been walking around the fair hoping to convince someone to help. "If I don't find her a home today, I'll have to take her back to the shelter and they'll kill her," the woman told me. I was not in the market for another cat—I had four other rescued cats already, one of whom was undergoing chemotherapy and another fearful one who was being victimized by the remaining two. But I couldn't say "no" to a tiny baby in need.

The woman provided me with nothing but food and a carrier. It was in the 90s that day, and I was stuck in my booth for another seven hours until the fair closed for the night. A couple of my customers came to the rescue: they convinced a local pet supply store to loan me a litter box and litter, as well as a water dish. After the young woman left, I realized that the kitten was very sick. She was skinny, covered in fleas, sneezing, and very lethargic. I named her Tallulah Jane, thinking that this six-week-old kitten needed an oversized name to grow into. My plan was to nurse her back to health and then find her a new home.

When the fair closed, I drove straight to an emergency vet, where they diagnosed her with an upper respiratory infection. I kept her quarantined in my bathroom and took her in for frequent checkups with my regular vet, but Tallulah's condition only got worse over the next few weeks. She dropped below one pound and was almost completely unresponsive; she wouldn't even open her eyes. When my vet's response was, "Kittens are resilient; she'll be fine," I changed vets. I could see that Tallulah was dying. My new vet characterized her as a "fading kitten" and immediately started her on subcutaneous fluids, syringe-feeding, and multiple medications. She also began seeing a veterinary eye specialist. The diagnosis was a chronic case of feline herpes virus, which caused corneal ulcers that were damaging her vision. At one time she was on as many as nine different medications—some had to be administered every four hours around the clock, some were two or three times a day, others were once a day but had to be twelve hours apart from another once-daily medication. Some were given orally and others had to be put in her eyes. Some required refrigeration and one even had to be kept frozen. I created a three-page spreadsheet to track her treatments, and took time off work to care for her.

When I finally had to go back, I arranged to come into the office late and leave early, and I had a friend come in while I was gone to make sure Tallulah got all her medications. Her recovery had its ups and downs; an MRI confirmed that the virus had actually eaten away some of the bony structures in her sinus cavity. She would never completely recover, but her condition could be managed.

Tallulah Jane

By the time Tallulah Jane was well enough to come out of quarantine after three months, she and I had bonded and there was no longer any question that she was mine and I was hers. She had grown into a gorgeous cat with a plush coat. I had begun taking her to vet appointments in a carrier styled like a shoulder bag, open at the top so she could look out. Nothing seemed to frighten her as long as she was with me. So I started bringing her with me when I ran errands, and she continued to enjoy those outings.

In 2004, I took a chance and brought her to a benefit event where I was selling my art and donating a portion of the proceeds to a cat rescue group. I put Tallulah's bed on my table, and she calmly hung out there and greeted my customers. She was such a hit that I sold more than usual! After that I began bringing her to every event where pets were allowed, so long as the time frame was no more than eight hours. Tallulah gained quite a fan base, and people would come up to me at events and ask for her if she wasn't there.

In 2011, I noticed that Tallulah no longer seemed to be enjoying those outings. She started just sleeping through the events instead of engaging with the people who came to see her. So I decided to let her retire from her art assistant gig, and I've gotten a new rescued kitten, Saffron, who is being trained to replace her.

Tallulah now spends her days snuggling up with her best friend Annabel (another rescued cat) and playing with her other feline siblings. She still needs daily treatment to control her illness, but her symptoms are well managed and she's a happy little girl. I love all my cats, but I have to admit that Tallulah holds a special place in my heart that no one else can touch.

Tallujah (left) and her soul mate, Annabel.

Leslie Cobb
San Lorenzo, CA

Loose "Lucy" Caboose

Although through the years I have rescued many, and been rescued by as many more, the story of Lucy's amazing recovery is always one of my favorites. To say that I rescued Lucy isn't quite accurate. In truth, she found me by some miraculous method known only to cats. It was late in February 2004 and everything was covered in an icy mess and was very cold. One morning my husband went out to the driveway to warm up the car and came back in to report that he heard a cat under the car. I hurried out and sat on the cold driveway and called "kitty kitty kitty," and a moment later a small black cat dragged herself into my lap, mewing piteously. She smelled absolutely horrid; it was the smell of rot and infection that I had learned so well when I had worked for a veterinarian early in our marriage. She was just bones with skin on them and unable to walk properly. I gathered her into a large towel and took her inside. I offered small amounts of water and just a bit of food; she was starved, but I knew that too much in that emaciated tummy would come back up. I bundled her into one of our carriers and we dropped her at a vet's office near our office in town.

Later that day, I received a call from the vet that the kitten had a broken hip and pelvis that had already healed in a turned way, which had eliminated her ability to deliver her litter. They were all dead and rotting inside of her. She was so starved and weak that surgery would kill her. We opted for oxytocin injections, and by the end of the day the babies were out of her. They gently cleaned her up and medicated her and we picked her up on the way home. She spent the next two months of her life in a large cage in the family room. She had to be kept quiet and eased into eating like a normal cat. All of her hair fell out from the malnutrition. Her broken pelvis and hip would have to stay the way they had healed. The vet felt it would be cruel and unsuccessful to rebreak it to correct it.

Each evening I would take her gently from her bed and hold her against my body and stroke her so she would know human touch and love. She was the size of a two- or three-month-old kitten. Over the months she had multiple dewormings, one-at-a-time vaccinations, and triumphantly, a successful spay. Slowly her hair grew back, thick, black, and lustrous. She gained strength and coordination and can now go up and down steps, jump into my chair with me, and even run down the hall (although comically). She bonded to me so solidly that she rarely leaves my side and purrs when she sees me. She is even a bit jealous of the others that have joined our family. I just remind her that some moved over to allow her into our family, and she must do the same now.

When Lucy goes up and down the steps, her right rear leg only touches down every other step. She has a cute little comical walk from behind; because of that, my husband named her Loose Caboose, but we usually call her "Lucy."

One evening as I sat holding this baby to soothe her, she began chewing on my new glasses, which I had hanging on a chain around my neck. Since they were expensive, I just reached down to extricate them from her mouth, and YOW she caught my middle finger on my right hand in a very hard crunch, right through the top knuckle and the tendon. I cleaned it and treated it, but by the next morning it was swollen to the elbow and excruciating. I am deathly allergic to almost all antibiotics, so my doctor was hard put to treat me. I spent two months on the only antibiotic I can take, which was not very effective against cat bacteria. My entire right hand curled into a claw; there was debate about removing the arm at the elbow, and later at the wrist, and finally just the finger. (I type on a computer for a living; these were NOT options.) I soaked and vomited and missed a lot of work, but finally the infection healed. I was left with two crippled fingers, which after two more months of physical therapy returned to 90% use-ability. So as Lucy healed, so did I, and we did it together in this big old recliner.

Lucy looking beautiful.

I really make an effort to treat all my fur babies equally, but sometimes that extra bonding occurs due to all the extra handling and care that a really needy one requires. Lucy rarely leaves me and constantly stays close by me. She stays on the arm of my chair with or without my attention. She does show jealousy whenever a new one requires any extra time and attention. When she chose me, I had another very special kitty and he taught her how to sleep on my back (I am a tummy sleeper). Those two would take turns purring on my back; it was like built-in massage therapy! She is one that would have died for certain, so our bond is a little deeper.

Cheryl Veazey
Linwood, KS

Follow Lucy and her siblings on their Facebook page: https://www.facebook.com/pages/Meet-My-Five-Kitties/160960110639568

Coco

As an adult, I was owned by two cats. One, Oreo. I chose her out of a litter of kittens in August of 1987. My second cat, Cookie, I rescued from certain death in 1990, as a friend of mine was about to take him to a "farm" to live. He was most certainly too tiny to be on his own at a farm so I rushed him off to the vet and he became my second child! Oreo succumbed to illness in August of 2001 and left me bereaved. I lost my Cookie, in September of 2006. I was heartbroken a second time. I told my husband that I just couldn't go through another loss like that. My cats were the children I never had. I missed my little ones greeting me at the door each time I arrived home.

In the late evening of July 2, 2007, my husband was on his way home from work on highway M-46. It was a very warm night. It was dusk when he noticed a "leaf" in the road up ahead. The "leaf" suddenly had little eyes looking right at him. He slammed on his brakes, but it was too late. He knew he had gone over the little kitten in the roadway but wasn't sure if he had actually run it over. He was the only car on the road at the time so he opened his door to get out and see what he'd done and before he could put his feet on the ground, out came the little tiny kitten from underneath the car. He had stopped right over top of the tiny little kitten and had not hurt it. He picked up the kitten and went house to house to try to see if the kitten belonged to anyone, but of course, no one in the tiny little town would claim it.

He called me to tell me he was bringing a kitten home and would I run out and get some food and litter. He said the kitten wasn't in very good shape and thought it had fleas. I told him to go ahead and bring it home and I would have a place ready for it, but that we were not going to keep it. When he got the kitten home we tried to feed it, but it wouldn't eat. I tried the "kitten milk" from the store, as well as water, and then just regular milk. It lapped up a little bit but that's all. I thought the poor kitten was going to die during the night. We made a bed in the cat carrier and left it food and water. I told my husband he'd have to call the vet in the morning to see if he could get it in. It had fleas and ear mites as well as fluid draining from its eyes and nose. I could only imagine what else the poor thing might have.

Low and behold the kitten was still with us in the morning and a trip to the vet changed her life. She had a respiratory infection, worms, ear mites, and fleas, but the vet said she was pretty strong to make it through all of that. He thought she might be about four weeks old. She came through the ordeal with flying colors and was a wild and crazy kitten, climbing up curtains and people. She liked sitting on my husband's shoulders to survey her new surroundings.

Still reluctant to keep her, I told my husband he'd have to find her a home. Well, every time he came to me with someone that said they wanted her. I said no. She was pretty wild and I thought it would have to be someone that would tolerate her being so wild and I didn't want to give her to someone that might give her away or worse, just let her out to be on her own again. After about six weeks I finally told him that I just couldn't give her away. As wild as she was, she tugged at my heart and even though she really was attached to my husband, I just couldn't let her go. We gave her the name Coco because of a brownish spot on top of her head that looked like someone spilled cocoa on her head. She will flip the light switches off and on and occasionally knock the thermostat off the wall. She still chases headlights across our wall when a car turns the corner near our house, and occasionally will run and perform a half flip in the hallway. She is and will always be part of our family. She has no interest in going outside at all. We purchased a pet stroller and tried taking her outside, but she is terrified of the sound of cars driving by.

I now know that I have plenty of room in my heart for Coco, and just last November we added Rascal to our house. He's also a rescue, but that's another story. Our lives have certainly changed. My husband is now a "cat" person too and feels very responsible for her life.

Sue
Saginaw, MI

Coco all grown up.

119

Steffy

It all started out with Prissy. My vet said I needed to start feeding her soft food, so I started feeding her a can of Fancy Feast classic chicken, which she gobbled up. Great! So I went and bought a case. She wouldn't touch it. Confused, I went to the Fancy Feast Facebook page and asked if there was any difference between buying by a single can and a case; I already knew the answer (there is no difference), but asked anyway. Someone named The Grannies also commented on the reply post.

Intrigued, I went to The Grannies Facebook page. I liked what I saw, especially the pictures of sweet senior kitties Juliet (spokescat for The Grannies) was trying to find homes for. One really touched my heart; a woman named Rachel said she had seen this old cat wandering her neighborhood, and then on one particularly scorching Texas afternoon, the flea-ridden, matted, mite-infested little girl collapsed at her feet. She scooped up the poor cat and rushed her to the vet, where she was cleaned up, proclaimed toothless, "ancient", and in need of a hospice home. She also had an old hind-end injury received when she was hit by a car; it resulted in her walking with a peculiar shuffle. She is also deaf. The vet believed she wouldn't live past three weeks.

Her cute little face and her very sad story touched my heart, so I decided to give her the best life I could for her remaining time; the sweet senior kitty deserved it. My heart broke and I cried, vowing to give Steffy the best home for her last days.

Rachel and I messaged back and forth for a couple of days to get things coordinated. I drove the 100 miles to Austin to get her, and when we met, Rachel wanted to make sure Steffy liked me and that Steffy would be safe. It took about 20 minutes for Steffy to warm up to me, and Rachel also figured I was OK as her other kitties hovered around me! On the ride home, Steffy "gracked"—her version of mew—for about half an hour. Whether it be for riding in a car or missing Rachel, I'm not sure. A short time later she got up in the passenger seat and I reached over and gently stroked her head and talked to her, even though I knew she couldn't hear. After about another 15 minutes, she fell asleep and slept almost the rest of the way home.

When I got Steffy home, I took her straight to my vet, where they found more evidence of her old injury as well as a severe case of arthritis and degenerative joint disease. She was treated by some of the best vets, made more comfortable, and returned home with a regimen of medicines and treatments. My life is a bit different having Steffy because of her conditions. I suppose I am overly protective of her, as I don't trust too many to look in on her and see to her needs. I get far more back from Steffy than I give to her. She gives me love, companionship, and laughs (some of her antics are very funny). She has a feather toy she loves and looks like a kitten when playing with it.

The very pretty Steffy.

I shudder to think where Steffy would be if Prissy hadn't turned her nose up at the Fancy Feast. I wouldn't have found The Grannies and thereby Steffy. She and Prissy helped me get through losing my sister in Thanksgiving of 2011, and Steffy really helped me get over losing Prissy in 2012.

So, would I do it again? In a second.

Bob
College Station, Tx

Krumpet

My rescue was Krumpet. Krumpet was one of a litter of three girls. Their mother brought them to my house one day when they were small, and then sadly she was killed a few days later. Krumpet would bring her two sisters to my house every day to eat. She was outside for over a year and ended up pregnant. Right before she had her kittens, she ran inside and adopted me. I'm not sure if she had a home or was a stray, but once she came in she didn't care about going back outside.

It worked out, because we were moving and couldn't just leave them there. We found homes for her two sisters, and Krumpet stayed with me until Jan 19, 2012, when she passed away in her sleep from old age—almost 14 years old.

Krumpet's winning photo entry from Santa's cutest helper pet contest in December 2011.

Krumpet was different from any other cat I ever had. She knew when something was wrong. If I was crying or didn't feel well, she would stay with me until I told her I was OK. She was smart and always knew what was happening. Once when there was a problem with the furnace she woke my mother by tapping her till she woke up. The firemen said they arrived just in time. A little while longer and the furnace would have blown up.

When we were moving, everyone said that we wouldn't be able to get Krumpet in the carrier, but when it was time to go, she walked right into the carrier and waited to leave. I closed the door and she sat in there waiting for about two hours and never cried or meowed. Krumpet was always with me and was always checking on me to see what I was doing and if I needed her.

Krumpet

Cindy
Hanover Township, PA

Check out Krumpet's family on their Facebook page: https://www.facebook.com/pages/Dot-and-Family/301029486621771

Stevie Houdini Carpet Cat

I really don't know where to start with our story about Houdini. His past is kind of vague, so I'll start at our beginning with him.

My husband and I had been without a cat for a couple of years after having cats all of our lives. Then one day I saw a picture on the internet of a scared looking kitty with marble blue eyes looking at me from inside a cage. It seemed like he was waiting for us. He looked to be a full-bred Norwegian Forest Cat. The only trouble he seemed to have was his blindness (which we later found out was due to neglect). We were in love. We had to get this cat!

Our challenge, though, was that he was in North Carolina and we live in Illinois. I asked my husband if he would like to take a trip to get a cat. He said of course! Two days later, we were on our way to get him. We finally arrived at the shelter and there he was waiting for us. We filled out the paper work and off we went with our new family member. It was a long ride home and he was very scared, but when we got home he changed completely. Once he found his way around the house and found the food, he was the king of the castle. He has been an important member of our family ever since.

Houdini's rescuer had named him Stevie. We decided we wanted to name him Houdini, so we just added it to Stevie and he became Stevie Houdini. We added

Stevie Houdini Carpet Cat

124

Carpet Cat because he doesn't have to walk in a metal cage anymore, he walks on fluffy carpet. Add it all together and his official name is Stevie Houdini Carpet Cat.

His blindness does not keep him from doing whatever he wishes. He does have some health issues that we deal with once in a while, but he is well worth it. He has been the sweetest, gentlest cat we've ever had. He has his snuggle time with me every night. He insists! I would highly recommend that if a rescue cat or dog is in anyone's future, that they look into adopting a special needs pet. They have so much to share with us. They need us and truly give back in so many ways. We wouldn't trade our time with Houdini for anything.

Julie Wetzel
Urbana, Illinois

Houdini is six years old and is one of Lola's best friends.

Priku

It was a sunny day in August 2008, when my boyfriend got a phone call from his mother. There was a very tiny little kitty in a fabric store, and my boyfriend's sister was going to go and pick it up. We decided to go to help her since we lived very close to the shop, but when we arrived there, there was no sign of the little kitty. We looked everywhere but couldn't find it. The shop owner told us that when she came in that morning, she had seen something tiny running under the shelves and thought it was a mouse. So she took a broom and tried to get it out. But then she realized, it was a tiny little black kitten!

Since there was nothing that we could do, we went back home. Later that day we got another phone call from my boyfriend's mother. The kitty had been found and it was at my boyfriend's parents' house, so we went there that evening. The kitten was very scared so it was in the shower room, but I had to see it. There it was: a very black little furry ball in the back of a carrier. It hissed and growled at me and looked at me with very big eyes. I was in love! I knew we were meant to be together. I just fell in love that very first second that I saw it. I had to have it. I had to....

The kitten was at my boyfriend's parents' house for six days. The shop owner did ask her customers if they knew whose cat it was, but no one knew. First my boyfriend thought it wouldn't be possible because we had a chinchilla, but then we thought that since the cat was a little kitty, maybe it will understand that the chinchilla isn't food, that it is a family member.

One beautiful day later we got our baby. My boyfriend gave it the name Priku (Finnish for Spotty) because it had a little white spot in its chest. We didn't know was it a boy or a girl, so the name was very good. But it was still a very scared little kitty! It lived the first weeks in our spare room, hiding under a computer table. Every time we went to see it, it hissed and growled at us. But it ate well and even used a litter box.

After two weeks, we finally got Priku out from under the computer table with a toy. Priku was still a little scared, but curiosity won. When it was no longer scared of us, we took it to the doctor to get the first vaccinations. The doctor told us that it was a boy! When our little boy was old enough, we got him neutered. When he was a year old we decided he needed another cat to be his friend. He started to clinging to me too much, so we got a little girl kitty. When my boyfriend and I broke up he was nice enough to let me have the cats because he knew how much I loved them.

Priku is a special cat because he does not know how to meow. Maybe it is because he was so tiny when we found him and his mother didn't get the chance to teach him.

Or maybe someone abused him. I won't ever know the real reason, but I will always love him and I think that his different talking just makes him so special.

Priku was my first cat. We never had a cat when I was a child, but I thought it would be nice. When I started dating my boyfriend (his parents and sister had cats), that feeling grew. When we got Priku, I didn't know much about cats, but I learned a lot. They are so amazing; I can't imagine my life without them. When I come home from work, my little furry babies are waiting for me in corridor. I have been called a crazy cat lady, but I carry that name proudly.

When you save an abandoned animal, you get so much. It's an amazing feeling, when you finally get their trust. Priku still is scared of new people, but getting braver every day.

And no, black cats are not bad luck!

Marianne
Finland

Priku (left) and Killi.
(Killi was adopted from a shelter)

127

Napoleon

I have been a volunteer at Anjellicle Cats Rescue in New York City at their "cat room" shelter on West 49th Street for over four years now. Despite having three cats at the time, in the early fall of 2009 I was intrigued by a stocky black-and-white cat that had an unusually calm and dignified demeanor despite the cramped, chaotic environment that it was in. I didn't know what the cat's name was or even if it was a boy or a girl, but after seeing it a few times over the course of a month or so, I said to myself, "If it is still there next time I come, I will ask about it." Two weeks later this chill, big-headed cat was still hanging out at the shelter, so I snapped a picture of it and sent it to the volunteer coordinator. I got a message back telling me his name was Brendan. I thought this was a little strange, since Brendan isn't terribly common—and it's my little brother's name.

I don't know why I thought I would foster him, especially since I was already at cat capacity at my tiny studio apartment, but obviously I wasn't thinking clearly. When I went to pick Brendan up to bring him to his "foster home," I looked at him and the name Napoleon immediately popped in my head; he was standing there so regally, I knew he needed a proper aristocratic name.

Things didn't go very smoothly when I first brought Napoleon home. My other three cats were totally uninterested in having another friend and would hiss and growl at him constantly. But Napoleon was unfazed; he would literally stare at them for a second and then flop over wherever he was and take a nap. After about a month, the other cats stopped hating him and thereafter it soon became a love fest between Napoleon and the other boys Felix and Bali. My girl Matilda, who was originally a feral and then an only cat, has since learned to accept his presence even though she does not approve.

When I told my mother I was fostering Napoleon, she was completely horrified, chastising me over the phone for being a crazy cat lady and telling me how I wasn't allowed to bring any cats home that I volunteer with. I knew she was right, but there was also something else in me that knew Napoleon was special. After a few months, I received an email from Anjellicle asking for current photos so they could update his adoption profile. It was then I knew I couldn't let him go, despite the fact that he had given me ringworm.

When I received the ACC info sheet on him, I was surprised to find out that he was only three years old because he looked so much older (my mother told me he looked like he was ten). He must have had a hard-knock beginning, because he's got a mouth full of missing and broken teeth, but rest assured that doesn't stop him from eating as much as he can—he is quite the foodie.

It's somewhat difficult to articulate what is so extraordinary about him, but essentially every day with Napoleon is a total joy. He loves life, any type of toy, and sitting square in the middle of my chest whenever I am reading a book on the couch. He is constantly wagging his tail and cuddling with people or the other cats (excluding Matilda, since she doesn't allow that!). Countless friends and family members have literally begged me to let them take him; even non-cat lovers are immediately enamored of him.

Napoleon looking dapper.

He is just such a good guy; he always knows when someone is feeling down or sick and is right there to comfort them. This was particularly evident this past summer, when my cats were on vacation at my parents lake house. My mom was finishing up an intense round of chemotherapy and Napoleon was constantly with her. It was amazing to see what having a buddy to nap with and watch countless reruns of Law & Order did for her spirits! I'm pretty certain my parents are counting down the days until this summer when they can pick the cats up for "kitty camp" again.

Despite having a" foster that turned into an adoption" under my belt, I still volunteer at the same shelter and have since successfully fostered other cats (when mine were on vacation). I've learned that even little acts of kindness go a long way, and whether you are a volunteer, a foster parent, an adopter, or even a good Samaritan, it can make a huge difference in the lives of animals that had a rough start in life and need a fresh start.

Napoleon (left) with Bali, ultimate best friends.

Bridget Sweeny
New York, NY

Check out the adventures of Napoleon, Bali, and their siblings on their Facebook page: https://www.facebook.com/pages/Studio-54-Kittehs/228196157193474

Flipper and Bubba

I do Trap-Neuter-Return (TNR) with some friends, and one day they received a call about a mom cat and her day old babies, so they went with the special traps and got them. The feral mom cat was consequently fixed and released after her kittens were four weeks old. My friend fostered the kittens, who eventually were adopted out by the Humane Society—with the exception of the little special one with the crooked paws. He was given to me to babysit for a few days. He had a very strong tail and back legs and jumped like a kangaroo. He appeared on the kitchen table in seconds and wobbled over to my husband's cereal bowl, and they ate breakfast together. We fell in love with him and named him Flipper because of his crooked front feet.

After researching, we found out that he has radial hypoplasia, which means the bones in his front feet didn't fuse together. We took him to the doctor, who said they wouldn't be able to do anything for him. It is a condition he must live with for the rest of his life.

Well, nothing stops Flipper! He flies from the kitchen table to the couch like Superman and runs faster than lightning. Who cares if his feet look a little different? Flipper is like any other cat in the house and stands up for himself. He is very personable and loves to sit up on his back feet and beg for treats. I have met other cats on Facebook that share the same condition as Flipper. Flipper turned seven years old in May 2014, and I just love this boy.

Flipper dancing

I feed several feral cat colonies. Bubba, the buff-colored male cat, was trapped, fixed, and released back into the colony. He then disappeared for months. I looked around and called for him to no avail and then checked with another feeder in the area who I have helped TNR. He said Bubba would show up at his house once in a while but waited in the back until all the other cats were done eating, and he appeared very skinny. After coaxing him back to the colony, he would sit behind the chain link fence and just look at me. It was breaking my heart.

One cold evening while lying in bed, I was thinking about him and woke my husband up and insisted we go look for Bubba. He wasn't there that night, but the next day he was waiting for me and on my side of the fence! I grabbed him and placed him in a carrier. I contacted the Humane Society of Tampa Bay, who looked at him and said he had stomatitis (a severe, painful inflammation of a cat's mouth and gums) and suggested his teeth be removed; he had an eye infection as well.

Bubba had his teeth removed on December 23, 2010. After a few weeks of antibiotics, he improved and was like a new cat. He was eating wet food and started to gain weight. He lived in my cat house and was the door greeter to anyone coming in. I could tell he was so grateful for his new life. He never had to worry about getting into fights, and he slept like a baby. I know he was an older cat because of his issues. In January of 2013 Bubba collapsed in his potty box and was rushed to the ER vet. His temperature was very low, which meant his organs were shutting down. I needed more proof, and a blood test showed that he was in liver failure and much more. I was told he would never be able to turn around this

Beautiful Bubba

132

time. So with tears in my eyes I let him go to Heaven. We gave each other two wonderful years together. I changed his life and he changed mine.

Vicky Tillman
Tampa. FL

You can follow how Flipper is doing on Facebook: https://www.facebook.com/pages/Flipper/175237369197784

Cindi Lou

In May of 2010, my boyfriend and I were coming home one night and we saw a flash of something run across his yard. From what we could see, it was black and white, and we instantly assumed it was a skunk. We even laughed about it and said it was a good thing it didn't spray us. We kept a look out for the "skunk" just to make sure it was that indeed a skunk and not a cat.

A few days later, I went off to work and my boyfriend sent me a text saying, "I think we have a problem." I had no idea what he was referring to. The next text that came was a picture of this "skunk" scarfing down the food my boyfriend had given her. He took a video of her and she was meowing while eating her food as if say, "Mmmm, this is sooo good, nom, nom, nom, thank you!" At this time, I had just bought a house and already had three rescued cats at home; I just wasn't financially able to take on another cat. I tried to find a home for her and almost had one—until we found out she was pregnant. She was not getting along with the dog and most pregnant cats are quite grumpy and protective, so she wasn't making for a good pet. I dropped her back off at my boyfriend's

Cindi Lou when she was rescued.

house, not sure what to do. I looked out the window one day and saw her sleeping right outside the window in the dirt. This was breaking my heart.

The next day I came over to check on her and couldn't find her. I looked and looked and started to panic. I looked everywhere and even ran over to the Bay County Animal Control to see if the neighbors took her there. Thankfully, she wasn't there. Finally, after about two hours of searching for her, she strolled up slowly and laid down panting. It was June and pretty warm that day. Not knowing anything about pregnant kitties, I thought she was hot. I decided right then and there to take her home and put her in my upstairs spare bedroom so I could make sure she was OK. I was so worried about her and I was thinking she's getting heat stroke! Like I said, I was not familiar with pregnant kitties.

Cindi Lou today.

135

I took her home right then. No carrier, nothing. Just put her in the back seat and told her everything was going to be OK. She seemed to think differently and told me so all the way home. I took her upstairs to my spare bedroom away from my other kitties. That night we had a horrible thunderstorm. I remember thinking; thank God I brought her home. I named her Cindi after Cindy Crawford because of her little back dot by her nose. Cindi Lou came next just because it flowed. The next morning I had to leave very early and decided to check on her before I left. Bad news awaited me, Cindi Lou had miscarried her two babies, which is why she was panting. She was in labor and I didn't know it, and the babies did not make it to full term. She was grooming them and nudging them and it broke my heart. I called the vet that morning and made an appointment to get her in and get checked to make sure she didn't have any unborn babies left. I also had her tested for Feline Leukemia and Feline Aids. More bad news: Cindi Lou came back positive for Feline Leukemia. Apparently, a symptom of Feline Leukemia is that pregnant kitties will miscarry their babies.

I was devastated. The vet that I went to at that time pretty much gave her a death sentence and said it was normal procedure to put them down, because there is no hope for them, that they don't live long, and that I shouldn't keep her in my home and put my healthy kitties at risk. I'm standing there bawling, and I look down and here is this adorable tiny friendly kitty looking up at me and purring like crazy as if to say, "Take me home Mom, I promise I'll be good." I wiped my tears and I said to the vet, "Well it's a good thing I don't follow the norm." With that, I scooped her up and took her home.

She does have a home and has her own room, the Penthouse Suite (as Cindi Lou refers to it on her Facebook page, where she helps raise awareness about Feline Leukemia and that it isn't a death sentence). For a while she shared her room with her sibling, Harriet, who also had Feline Leukemia but succumbed to the disease. She has a brother Tipsy who has Feline Leukemia, too. Cindi Lou and Tipsy are doing great and show no signs of the illness. I also have found a new vet.

There is a lot of information on Feline Leukemia on the Internet and I have read hours and hours of it. Although it can take a cat's life earlier than expected, they can also live long happy healthy lives with a healthy diet and lots of love.

Sherri Howell
Bay City, Michigan

You can follow Cindi Lou and Tipsy on their Facebook pages:
https://www.facebook.com/pages/Cindi-Lou/183482885009711?fref=ts
https://www.facebook.com/TipsyTheTripod?fref=ts

Trooper Hawkings

Trooper was a stray kitten who was bitten pretty severely by a dog. The dog's owner kept Trooper in the garage for four days before she finally did the right thing and dropped him off at Felines, Inc., a no-kill shelter in Chicago, Illinois. The dog's owner did not tell them what was wrong with Trooper because she was afraid of what would happen to her dog. Regardless, the director Abby thought he was born that way and upon further examination found out it was a dog bite.

Abby looked into his eyes and saw that he wanted to live. He was just a sweetheart to everyone he met. Even though he couldn't walk, he dragged himself to the litter box and purred nonstop. He had surgery to repair the puncture wounds, his intestines, and a hernia, but the vet felt he would make a full recovery. He had three weeks of cage rest so that he could heal. The shelter had their Facebook fans come up with a

Trooper and his new mom.

137

name for him. They decided on Trooper because after all he went through he is a trooper, and Hawkings because of Stephen Hawkings the brilliant scientist. Even at this point, however, no one was still 100% sure he would make a full recovery.

On November 9th I adopted him.

He is a fully recovered and rambunctious kitten. He has three siblings: Mac, 3 years old; Zoey, 5 years old; and Mudpie, 15 years old. Mac has adopted Trooper as his brother, taking him under his wing from the second day he got here. Trooper has transformed our home from a loving one to a magical one.

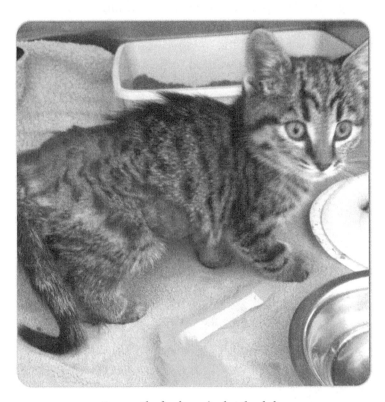

Trooper the day he arrived at the shelter.

He was such a sought-after kitten that I made the decision to start a Facebook page for him so everyone at the shelter could be a part of his story. In fact he inspired me so much that I will be going to work for the shelter that saved him.

Paula A. Grabow
Chicago, IL

Follow Trooper on Facebook: https://www.facebook.com/TrooperHawkins?fref=ts

Studley

My wife, Pam, volunteers at Animal Services, the local shelter and service organization supported by Olympia, Lacey, Tumwater, and Thurston Counties, here in Washington State. While working with cats there in early 2006, she met a cat who was a rescue found along a country road and who appeared to have not eaten in at least two weeks. His long white coat was matted, and he only weighed about 4½ pounds. He had acute gingivitis, and his prognosis wasn't good. He could barely stand, but wobbled over to Pam and her heart was touched. She started to try and remove his matted pieces of fur, but could not get everything before her shift ended. She brought me back the next day and both of us worked to clean him up a little. We talked with staff there and decided to foster him, to bring him back to health since he would probably otherwise be euthanized.

After he made his first visit to a vet and was neutered, he was brought home. He mostly slept and kept close to us. He was happy to get food and eat well. He was home for over three weeks before he first tried to play with a toy. It was a happy moment, because it was the first time he started to act like a happy cat and look like he would thrive.

We adopted him in April 2006 and named him Studley to give him a strong name to live up to, and he has done so! We started to take him with us in the car frequently, and on visits to PetSmart he would sit calmly in the shopping cart and let people pet him who passed by and admired his two colored eyes, one deep blue and the other sparkling amber. He would also accompany us to get coffee and would sit outside with us while we had coffee, where he got admired and petted by passers-by. Because of him, we began to learn more about cats and identified him as a Turkish Angora. His fur thickened into a fluffy long white coat.

Later in the summer of that year, there was a wellness fair at my office and one of the staff who had attended brought me a pamphlet from one of the exhibitors. It was about a program at Providence St. Peter's Hospital in Olympia, Washington, called the Providence Animal Assisted Activities and Therapy (PAAA/T) program. It was for animal-human teams to visit patients while they were in the hospital. It looked like something Studley could do, so Pam contacted the program coordinator and we learned that the next class for participants would start the following spring; we signed up to be on the waiting list.

As part of that program, we each had to become registered Delta Society Pet Partners and each pass a skills and aptitude test with Studley. He more than did his part in each test. We began visiting on the Psychiatric Unit in September 2007 and have continued to visit there approximately twice each month. Studley is required to have a bath within 24 hours preceding each visit, so that limits the number the times we can visit. He doesn't mind baths at all, but the process of drying him can be a little lengthy! During every visit he is calm and responsive to the petting and visiting. After we leave the facility, he is energized and seems very happy with himself. He knows when he is working and is proud afterward. We have attended many events and fairs with him, taking our turn at a shift in the PAAA/T booth. He has had the hands of many children on him at one time, always remaining calm and appreciative of the attention.

Studley's trading card.

Studley's visits to the Psychiatric Unit have been very beneficial to the patients and the staff there. Staff have told us many times of people who had been somewhat reclusive or quiet who had spoken and opened up for the first time when he was visiting. We have encountered a couple of occasions where Studley stared fixedly at someone who we thought didn't want to interact. Following his lead, we have approached the person and asked if they would like to visit him, and their whole demeanor changes and they open up like a bloom.

Once a nurse on the unit asked us to visit a patient in his room. This is very unusual, because our visits are usually limited to the day room area. The nurse accompanied us to the room where the patient was being watched by another nurse. He looked wary and cautious, but was interested in Studley. We approached and he began to slowly pet Studley and talk to him. In his usual fashion, Studley was obviously appreciative of the attention and responded to the petting. After we left the room, the nurse told us that they had mentioned the visiting cat to this patient. He was interested but was certain that the cat would have nothing to do with him. He believed the cat would be afraid of him. The nurse, however, had seen Studley in action many times and believed otherwise. That visit made a huge difference to that patient, whose own feelings of unworthiness were overcome for that visiting moment.

We have had many occasions where we have seen a patient again, months later, and they always remember Studley by name and sight. His ability to impress is truly impressive, and it constantly reminds us of the power of the human-animal connection.

Studley is the only cat in the program at the hospital. There are over 40 teams, but the rest are dogs. In speaking with Delta Society staff, the last we heard we are the only registered cat team in the Puget Sound area. We both believe that more cats could do this work but people just don't think of cats this way.

Studley greeting a fan.

Pam and Keith Phillips
Olympia, WA

Follow Studley on Facebook:
https://www.facebook.com/pages/Studley/211721135516488

Diamond

I was feeding a friend's cats and dogs while she was away in California for three weeks. Things were going smoothly until the last week. On the morning of May 24th, I walked up to her front porch and noticed a blue blanket lying on the steps. Then I saw a sticky note on the front door that read: "Dear Ola I found this cat. He is abandoned and was abused. He is hurt on his front leg. I thought you could take care of him." She listed her address with an arrow pointing in the direction of where she lives and noted "PS I am 13." I thought "OK, a 13-year-old is probably not going to realize the cat isn't going to hang around." I searched the bushes and didn't see anything, so I went to work. After work I went back by to let the dogs out and to search for this cat. This time when I walked up to the front door there was a cat sitting on the step that I didn't recognize. He was covered in scabies and couldn't move his eyes. He just sat there and cried at me. I rushed to get a carrier and coaxed him in and off to the vet I went.

Diamond when he was rescued and after he recovered

The vet and his staff were horrified at the sight of this poor cat, who they estimated to be approximately five years old. He immediately was given fluids for dehydration, had a depo-antibiotic shot, was treated with Ivermectin for scabies, and put on an antibiotic for 10 days. He had abscesses on his front legs and could hardly move any part of his body. He weighed 6 pounds, 9 ounces. He was dirty, his skin was matted hard from the scabies, and you could feel his backbone when you petted him. I took him home and syringe-fed him for days. I got him A/D wet food (which is often given to animals recovering from serious illnesses) and "Rebound" milk. I also gave him Nutrical, fish oil, and Lysine. He had his own little medicine cabinet! My husband named him Diamond because he had what looked like a diamond on his head—and he was a diamond in the rough. The vet had me bathe him in Selsun Blue and use a nail brush to get the gunk off him. After all that, he seemed to feel so much better! He was still very weak and had a hard time standing on his own, but he was so grateful and lovable.

After a week, he was much more stable and started eating on his own. He was getting fluids every other day and even received a vitamin B shot. His eyes started to open, and the scabies were falling off his ears and his body. We decided to have him tested and we were all on pins and needles, but thankfully he tested negative for Feline Leukemia and FIV. We were thrilled. Two weeks later, he was given his second Ivermectin treatment but was also running a fever, so he was put on another antibiotic and was given a second bath for the scabies.

Every day we see improvement. His scabies are almost gone and the abscess is starting to heal. He eats on his own and has gained 2 pounds. He purrs and now rolls over for petting. The vet is guessing he is about 6 years old.

Because he is so loving I know he was around people, but how he got in this horrible state I have no idea. His previous owners never even got him fixed.

Vicky Tillman
Tampa FL

Author's note: Diamond was adopted by one of Flipper's Facebook friends! You can follow his updates at https://www.facebook.com/pages/Diamond/581585695218161

Larry

Cats—I could take them or leave them, I thought. Until a feral mom had kittens under our deck and then left them on their own after a few weeks. One August day, my husband Steve came into the house with a tiny orange kitten. The kitten was feisty but couldn't get a sound out, no matter how hard he tried. We offered him some milk and he drank hungrily. We put him back under the deck, only to encounter him again the next day. Again, we fed him, but this time we decided to do more. He stayed in the house.

Steve left on a business trip the next day, and since I was on vacation that week, I had lots of time to spend with the kitty. He was a charmer but was covered with fleas. Holding him carefully with one hand, I drove the few blocks to our local vet's office and got his first shots and asked about the fleas. They said he was too little for flea medicine, but the infestation was so bad that they gave me some Frontline and said to put two drops of it on his back. Back at home, I carefully held him on my lap with a paper towel handy and administered the two drops. Within minutes, fleas started leaping off the kitten and onto my paper towel. Kitty looked up at me with grateful blue eyes, and in that moment I fell completely in love—totally and irrevocably IN LOVE!

Larry at home.

We named him Larry, as a reminder of the laryngitis he had that first day. By the time we caught his sister a month later, Larry was established as the ruler of the house. Now nine years later, Larry is the patriarch of our clan of seven cats. All the others should be thanking him daily, because if it hadn't been for Larry, none of them would be here with us. I wouldn't be a crazy cat lady, doing cat transports and cross postings. I wouldn't be a true CAT MOM, and my life would not be nearly as full of love. So who rescued who?

Linda Bee

Smoky

My husband and I are animal lovers, but never in my wildest dreams did I think I would adopt a cat. I am deathly allergic to cats. I love them, but I just can't be around them.

My life changed forever on Thanksgiving night 2007, however, when my husband befriended a cat in our neighborhood.

I call my husband Dr. Doolittle. He is a veterinarian by training and has this incredible effect on animals. When he walks down the street, all the animals come out of hiding to greet him—birds, squirrels, chipmunks, dogs, cats, even a turtle! It is like being in the middle of a Disney movie. This little cat came out of nowhere to greet my husband as he was bringing the trash out to the curb for our regular Friday pick up. He came running inside the house to get me. "You have to come see this cute little cat. She is adorable!"

I reluctantly went outside to meet his new friend. Despite my allergies, I could not resist this little cat. I picked her up, cuddled her, and brought her inside from the cold—I couldn't help myself! I knew my eyes would start watering, my throat would close up, and it would only be a matter of time before I would be scratching my entire body uncontrollably. But...it didn't happen. Of all the cats in the world, God brought a cat to my door that was hypoallergenic.

I had nothing to feed this cat but leftover turkey from our Thanksgiving feast. This was not roasted turkey, but smoked turkey. When you are hungry, you will eat anything. Needless to say, she gobbled it up. The cat was wearing a collar, but no identification tag. We were new to the neighborhood, so did not know if this kitty was just roaming the streets or was abandoned. We put her back outside in case she did belong to someone.

Over the next few days, I secretly hoped she would stop by the house for a visit. To my delight, she did. I was falling in love. We continued to feed her and to bond with her. I was amazed I was still not having any allergic reaction. I started calling her Smoky since her fur is black like smoke—and because of the smoked turkey.

The holiday weekend was coming to an end. We put up a "Found" sign on our neighborhood bulletin board. I added canned cat food to the grocery cart during my regular Sunday shopping trip. Monday came and it was time to go back to work. It was the longest day at the office. All I could think about was Smoky. I bought a litter box, litter, and more cat food on my way home.

My heart sank when someone responded to the "Found" cat notice. "What a beautiful cat, I'll take her." Oh thank goodness, this is not your cat, I thought to myself.

We had grown so attached to her. Smoky was OUR cat now. She didn't need a home. She already had one with us.

We took Smoky to the veterinarian for a complete checkup. Smoky was in excellent health, had been spayed, and was about a year old. She did not have a microchip, so there was no way to track and find her original owner.

There was an adoption event in progress when I stopped by the local pet supply store to stock up on food, litter, toys, and treats. There were several signs with fun facts to encourage black cat adoption. "A black cat goes with everything." "Holding a black cat is very slimming." "Black cats are always dressed for a formal affair." I was shocked to learn that the stereotypes and stigmas associated with black cats are still alive and well today in the United States. Many people consider black cats "unadoptable" because of the color of their fur. In many cases, black cats are first to be euthanized and the last to be adopted.

I just could not believe this and knew I had to do what I could to make a difference. I focused Smoky's social media channels on providing education to the public about black cats, helping black cats find their "furr"ever homes and raising money for some great cat nonprofit organizations across the country.

Smoky says Black Cats RULE!

Every year on Thanksgiving, we count our many blessings and celebrate Smoky's birthday. Even though the date changes from year to year, Thanksgiving was the first day this lucky black cat crossed our path.

Love knows no color.

Black Cats RULE!

Maureen Calloway Carnevale
Secretary to Smoky
Fairfax, Virginia

Follow Smoky on Facebook at https://www.facebook.com/Smoky.BlackCatsRULE and https://www.facebook.com/BlackCatsRULESociety

Sadie Mae McFlufferson

I have had many, many cats in my life, but Johnnie Cat was so full of personality, spunk, and pure love that his absence left a huge hole in my heart after he crossed the Rainbow Bridge. It seemed hard on our cat Samson as well, as he and Johnnie were the very best of friends. At that time, we had inherited Falkor, my daughter's cat, when she moved to Australia. Falkor was king of everything, everywhere, all the time. He was such a character, but he and Samson never clicked. And then, ten months after losing Johnnie, we lost Falkor. I was devastated. And Samson was very lonely. After a while, I finally decided it was OK to get another friend for all of us.

For years my husband and I had wanted a Ragdoll. We talked about it often, but we always brought cats home that someone else was trying to find homes for. Ragdolls are so beautiful and I had researched and learned a lot about their sweet, fun personalities, but I wasn't sure what path to take. So I decided that my first step would be to look and see if there were Ragdolls on any rescue sites. If there weren't, I made a final decision to look for any fluffy cat that needed a good home.

So I looked. And then—there she was! Her name was Lady Lovebug and I found her on Petfinder.com under a local rescue here in town.

The woman at the rescue named her Lovebug because of her loving personality. She had the most beautiful blue eyes I had ever seen. Her markings were a bit odd, with different color legs and she had the funniest crooked mustache. But her oddities are what drew me in. I was hooked. After talking to the rescue organization, I found out that somehow, this beautiful creature had started in Tennessee and ended up at the

Sadie Mae

149

local Humane Society. The shelter called the rescue to see if they wanted her. The rescue picked her up, got her vetted, and found a foster home for her. She was living in a nice home with dogs and two other cats. The foster family really wanted to keep her but they had a cat that did not like Lovebug and picked on her all the time. Sadly, Lovebug spent more time than not in a separate room.

I filled out the adoption application and waited. I held my breath and crossed my fingers that she was still available and that we would be accepted.

A week later, she was a new princess in our house. We were ecstatic! And she was even more beautiful than in her photos. The first night we set her up in my husband's office. We put everything she could want in there with her. We stayed with her until bedtime, but she made it very clear that she did not want to be locked in anywhere. So we let her out the next morning and she started her exploring. She adjusted to her new home and family almost immediately.

We renamed her Sadie Mae. Sadelle Mae McFlufferson. Sadelle, or Sadie, is a diminutive of Sarah, which means Princess in Hebrew. I had not had a female cat in over 25 years, so a princess was fine by me.

But then two days later, her energy level dropped. She started sneezing, her eyes watered, and she was scratching her ears. I called the rescue and she said to look everywhere on her body for any signs of a bite. She had seen situations where the existing cat would attack the new cat. I knew Samson didn't have a mean bone in his body, but upon inspection, my daughter and I found a very bad abscessed bite, under all that fluff, on her upper hind leg. We finally found out that the foster mom had heard a cat fight in another room just the day before Sadie Mae came to us and she had been previously treated for an ear infection. So after two trips to the vet and giving her medicine for the infection and her ears, we started the healing process. The upper respiratory issue ended up being an allergy to clay litter, which took a few days for me to figure out. But throughout all of this, despite her pain, Sadie Mae still had her sweet, playful, and loving personality.

Sadie loves to play fetch with toy mice, the small furry kind with the rattle inside. She goes crazy over the laser pointer and any Cat Dancer toy. Sadie loves a good party and will never turn down a niptini or tuna colada. In fact, she has yet to turn down any food or treat offered to her! She is a middle sister and keeps both of her brothers in line even thought they would never, ever admit it. And Sadie Mae is the main fluff of the McFlufferson's Fluffy Fluffs Facebook page. Sadie Mae is our pretty tomboycat. She's our mischievous princess in fluffylooms. She is our sweet and sassy southern belle. She makes me smile and laugh every day and has been such a joy. I'm so glad I was looking in the right place at the right time.

Beautiful Sadie Mae enjoying the sun

She most likely is not a pure Ragdoll; she could be a mix of Ragdoll and Birman. But it really doesn't matter what she is...because she's 100% fluffy Sadie Mae!

Jan McGinnis,
Ohio

Follow Sadie Mae and her siblings on Facebook at https://www.facebook.com/McFluffersonsFluffyFluffs

Althea

I was working as a teacher in the ghetto in East New York, Brooklyn. I would often see a friendly tabby cat on the street. I was very worried about her safety because she would cross Pitkin Avenue and trucks would come to a screeching halt to prevent hitting her. I knew it would be only a matter of time before she would be hit by a car. A kindly man, who ran the bodega across from the school where I worked would feed her but did not take care of her; she did not have a home.

One day, I approached her and "knew" she would be MY kitty. That day I decided to adopt her. I asked the bodega worker to keep her in his shop until I finished work. After work, I picked her up and discovered she was pregnant. I took her to a veterinarian, who found that she had several health problems: ringworm, bacterial infection in her ears, fleas, an infected paw (probably from a dog bite), a wound on her ear, and ear mites. The doctor came into the exam room wearing gardening gloves expecting her to be aggressive; however, Althea was the most docile creature! She was kept at the vet overnight so she could receive a flea bath and treatment for her health maladies.

Althea (top) and Blackie

In the morning when I picked her up, the staff was in love with her. They reported that she did not need any type of tranquilizer or gloves when given the flea bath. She just calmly allowed them to bathe her. They were amazed.

Two weeks after adopting Althea, she gave birth to six kittens. She was such a loving mom. She carried her babies throughout my apartment, piling them on top of each other for warmth and gently grooming them throughout the day. She also stayed near them and always watched them with a sharp eye.

We kept her son Blackie, a black-and-white cat with an adorable black chin. He was such a comedian. He fetched a ball, rolled up pieces of paper, gave paw, spoke on command, and NEVER hissed, scratched, or bit in his ENTIRE LIFE! He inherited his mother's temperament, at least that is what the vet often said. He adored his mother and would try to nurse from her, even as an adult. She would often give him a swat to show him that he no longer needed to nurse, yet he tried to nurse for 15 years. I have to admit it was funny to see a grown male cat, who outweighed his mom, attempt to nurse!

Althea was so graceful and unique. She loved being outdoors, and we bought a harness and went for walks. Everyone stopped us on the street and asked how we "trained" her to walk on a leash. We never trained her; she just walked and we followed her with the leash. When she approached a tree, we told her to "go scratch" and she would scratch her nails on the tree trunk.

I can fill up several pages with stories about them. They filled a void in my life and gave me the gift of friendship. I had their support through the good times and the bad. I held them while I cried as a seven-year relationship ended, when a dear relative died, through sicknesses, and other sad events. They were always there for me. Without trying to sound dramatic, they saved my life in more ways than one.

Please adopt a homeless cat. I can promise you that your life will never be the same again, and you will wonder how you ever lived without a kitty.

Emma Richman
Long Island City, NY

Tova

My Tova is a special dog. She only has three legs, but don't tell her. After previously adopting a dog with some special needs from our local dog shelter, we were contacted about a "big" black German Shepherd who had been surrendered as a cruelty case. We had a good reputation as pet owners/rescuers, as we had completely rehabilitated and trained our other rescued shepherd and we are foster parents for another local animal shelter, which had resulted in us having a previous dog with physical handicaps. Tova was rescued from a yard where she had been chained (literally with a big metal chain) with no food and no water. The chain had become wrapped around her leg and was causing her excruciating pain as it dug into her flesh. To free herself from the pain of being trapped, she was forced to chew her own leg off. When animal control was notified, they expected to find a dog with aggression issues due to pain. Despite hobbling

Tova with her favorite toy.

around the yard on her stump that was infected and had tissue reforming (meaning she had chewed her leg off at least a few weeks prior to her rescue), she was happy to see people. She allowed them to examine her leg while wagging her tail. They amputated the rest of her leg and spayed her before we were able to meet her. From the second I saw her first picture, I knew she would be perfect for me.

When we met her, she was nervous but sweet. She weighed 50 pounds and her coat was raggedy with plenty of dandruff. Her eyes were dull and she rarely made eye contact. But I couldn't have cared less and loved her immediately. I called my parents and explained the situation (I was a relatively poor graduate student) and my father paid her adoption fee for me as a Christmas gift that year and she was mine forever. From the first few days we had her, she would get overwhelmed by attention from us and the other pets in the house and she would need to "excuse herself" and go sit in another room by herself. After just a few short months, she learned how to cuddle with us and with her other furry siblings. She got a mischievous sparkle to her eyes. She also loves to "puppy punch" people to get their attention now. In a year, she has morphed into 80 pounds of a velvety, loving creature who likes to wear bandanas and ties, visit her grandparents, and lie in bed with me as long as I'll let her.

Tova the good and beautiful.

From a dog that started her life with no love and no attention and no training, she has blossomed into more than a pet. We have been working diligently with her so that she can take a test to become certified as a therapy dog, as we think her unique and forgiving personality and rough story would be an excellent therapy option for members of the military in the hospital. She knows to be gentle around seniors and children without our prompting. Never once has she retaliated toward humans or other animals. She has taught us that even though a dog might have a physical handicap, it does not mean they are any less of an awesome pet than any other animal. My house would not be complete without her (or my other dog or six cats and a turtle and fish). We are lucky to have rescued her, as she is both inspiring and motivational.

Who needs to a pay a breeder when you can get all that from a rescued pet?

Lyndsay Bottichio
Columbus, OH

Tova lives with her mommy and daddy Lyndsay & Tommy Bottichio and with her dog sister Zuorra, kitty siblings Kii, Bebe, Nicolai, Foofen, Dippy, and Quilty, turtle sibling Torit, and lots of fish friends (who she likes to stare at...very zen.) Tova's name is the Hebrew word for good and beautiful. She's a lucky dog and we are lucky parents.

Maddie Belle

Maddie Belle is my 8 pound, 14-year-old black Pomeranian who was born on December 21, 2000. Unfortunately she ended up in a puppy mill, which still exists and is only a few miles from my home. I have reported the mill with pictures and video. Our authorities did go and check things, but Louisiana law is not strict enough to allow them to confiscate the dogs, because in Louisiana dogs are considered livestock. The mill provides shelter and food but the law ignores the fact that the dogs live in 2 ft x 2 ft wire cages with another dog all of their lives. Maddie Belle was forced to have puppies whenever she was in season—twice a year for 12 years.

My friend Diana Gragston rescued Maddie Belle from her prison in 2012. Diana describes her as being covered in feces and fleas, and having urine-soaked, heavily matted hair. She took her to the veterinarian, where she was spayed and had a full dental. Diana thought Maddie Belle was dead at first because she lay on her side and didn't move. She would not eat or drink. She couldn't even lap water because her mouth was full of infection and rotten teeth. (All but three of her teeth were removed.) Maddie Belle was starving to death and was very dehydrated.

After the surgeries, Diana took Maddie Belle home and nursed her back to health. Diana said she had never seen a dog just lie on her side and not move for days. Maddie Belle's eyes were very cloudy, so Diana thought she was almost blind.

But as Maddie Belle's health improved, so did her vision. The poor nutrition in the mill had caused her teeth to rot and her eyes to grow cloudy. Plus, when she was pregnant she did not receive the proper diet; therefore, when she nursed her puppies, her calcium levels continued on a downward spiral. Diana cooked for Maddie Belle and gave her the love and nutrition she had been denied all of her life.

One day Diana met Ninna Thomas-Lopez. Ninna was opening a rescue for small dogs and older cats, and Diana asked Ninna to help her find Maddie Belle a forever home. In August 2012, I began volunteering at the rescue. Maddie Belle had been there for months, yet no one had shown any interest in adopting her. During my first day volunteering, Maddie Belle begged me to hold her. I held her for hours and fell in love. After talking with my family, I adopted her! She has changed my life.

Maddie Belle was very scared when I brought her home. She mostly just wanted to be held and had terrible separation anxiety. Maddie Belle would not lie down in my lap at first; she just sat like a little statue. Now she sleeps on the end of my recliner. She even snores sometimes! She doesn't give kisses, as she doesn't know how. She is a very picky eater and mostly just wants meat.

Maddie Belle has only snapped at me once. I was brushing her hair and the brush tugged on her hair. She is very sensitive about anyone touching her tail. And she fights like mad if I try to hold her like a baby on her back, so I don't do that nor do I let anyone else flip her over. Maddie Belle also has chronic stomach problems; puppy mill dogs develop ulcers from the stress of living in poor conditions, but her medical needs are easily managed.

Maddie Belle is starting to act more like a dog. She loves to chew bones even though she only has three teeth! I have purchased toys for her but she doesn't know what to do with them. Potty training was a breeze. She just followed my other dogs outside and copied their behavior! She is a very curious, spunky, sassy little girl who is full of personality. As she continues to relax in life, layers of her personality come through.

I have met so many people and made many friends, all because I adopted Maddie Belle. My dream of becoming involved with animal rescue has come to fruition! Maddie Belle and I are members of the Krewe of Barkus and Meoux, which is a Mardi Gras Krewe that supports rescues citywide. In October of 2012 she entered the Krewes' Halloween Costume Contest and won Cutest Costume. I was overjoyed. She had truly gone from rags to riches!

The gorgeous Maddie Belle

Maddie Belle is a working dog. She has her own Facebook page where she shares her views (with my help of course) on puppy mills, changing legislation regarding puppy mills, spaying and neutering, adopting older dogs, and adopting black dogs and cats. She also posts dogs and cats that are available for adoption. But her most important job is being the Ambassador to Ninna's Road to Rescue. She attends all adoptions and functions in which Ninna participates and also serves as a fundraiser for the rescue. She has been on local TV sharing her life and the importance of spaying and neutering.

Maddie Belle's motto is "Adopt, Don't Shop!" Puppy mills exist because they can be very lucrative. Her puppies were popular because black Pomeranians are rare. As long as her puppies were selling, she was made to have more.

Maddie Belle and I rescued each other. I cannot describe the love I feel for my girl. I have made a promise to Maddie Belle that she will never be put in a cage again. I had to break that promise when she was sick and had to spend the night at the vet. Seeing her in a cage with her back pressed up against the back wall as she trembled in fear was almost more than I could handle.

I tell Maddie Belle everyday "You are home, you are safe, I love you, and I will never leave you."

Nancy Miller
Benton, LA

Follow Maddie Belle on Facebook: https://www.facebook.com/MaddieBelleMiller

CPSIA information can be obtained at www.ICGtesting.com
Printed in the USA
LVOW03s0917011014

406728LV00006B/101/P